Choices for

An examination of the issue ̣_ʄʳ_*om*
the Housing (Scotland) Act 1988

Douglas S. Robertson

Scottish Council for Voluntary Organisations
18/19 Claremont Crescent
Edinburgh EH7 4QD

Published by the Scottish Council for Voluntary Organisations,
18/19 Claremont Crescent, Edinburgh EH7 4QD.

© *1992 SCVO*

ISBN 1 870904 35 4 paperback

Printed and bound in Scotland by Bell and Bain, Glasgow

Contents ■

LIST OF TABLES AND FIGURES

DEDICATION
To Anne, Niall and Jaime

ACKNOWLEDGEMENTS
The need for this publication, which examines the various options which arise out of the Government's latest piece of housing legislation, was made obvious to me by the substantial number of invitations to address tenants' meetings over the last three years. A general ignorance about the various implications of the legislation was also evident at training sessions for housing professionals and those with a professional interest in housing, whether they be lawyers, community workers, architects or builders. Hopefully this publication will help resolve many misunderstandings and allow those involved in the consequences of this legislation to make informed choices or offer accurate advice.

In drawing together the material for this publication I am indebted to a number of individuals for their assistance and advice. Could I therefore thank Sheila Adamson, Member Services Manager, Scottish Federation of Housing Associations; Greg Brown, Tenants Information Service; Jim Campbell, formerly Depute Town Clerk, City of Glasgow District Council; Chris Cunningham, Director, Shettleston Housing Association; Linda Ewart, Policy Officer, Scottish Federation of Housing Associations; Archie Fairley, formerly Director, Scottish Local Government Information Unit; Alan Ferguson, Lecturer in Housing, University of Stirling; Gerry Gormal, Chief Housing Officer (Area Renewal), City of Glasgow District Council; John Ross, Director, Whiteinch and Scotstoun Housing Association; Archie Stoddard, Assistant Policy Officer, Scottish Federation of Housing Associations; David Webster, Chief Housing Officer (Strategy and Research), City of Glasgow District Council; and Anne Yanetta, Lecturer in Housing, Edinburgh College of Art / Heriot-Watt University.

Could I also thank Ian Maxwell, of the Scottish Council for Voluntary Organisations for his assistance and help in the production of this publication. Given SCVO's commitment to providing easily understandable and comprehensive information for both the users and employees of the voluntary sector, it was the obvious organisation to approach to publish this material. Thanks also go to the University of Stirling for their financial assistance which allowed this publication to be competitively priced and thus more accessible to a variety of interested groups.

Can I also thank Sarah Pugh for typing the original report through its various drafts to this, its final form and Marion Morris for proofreading the final draft.

Finally, can I state that the views expressed within this publication are those of the author and not necessarily those of the Scottish Council for Voluntary Organisations.

*Douglas S. Robertson,
University of Stirling April 1992*

Introduction 1

This publication is specifically designed to provide a comprehensive overview of the various options which result from the Housing (Scotland) Act 1988 and its related counterpart, the Housing Act 1988. Although the latter deals mainly with England and Wales there are a few clauses which relate to Scotland. These in the main relate to voluntary transfers. It is written to assist and help all those who have an interest in public sector housing within Scotland, whether they be tenants or those with a professional interest or involvement in housing issues. Given the wide ranging changes which have been heralded in under this legislative framework it is perhaps surprising the lack of similar publications currently available. As a result, there are many people throughout Scotland who are presently being asked to make major decisions, which will not only affect their own future housing options, but also those of following generations, on the basis of very limited information. It is also often the case that those who offer advice, whether they be voluntary workers or an official of a district council or Government agency, do so from an equally uninformed basis. This publication will hopefully help fill this gap. There is, however, plenty of room for other publications, some of which may arise out of the questions and the interpretation of issues, thrown up by this book. Only with an adequate range of information is it possible for tenants to make informed choices. This is especially so given the complexities of this particular piece of housing legislation.

Following a brief exploration of the background to the current Scottish housing situation the book's first main task is to clearly outline the Government's objectives in promoting this legislation. Within this context, examination is made of the Government's desire to continue the spread of home ownership throughout Scotland. Their long standing commitment to revitalising the private rented sector is also explored. Consideration is then given to the Government's strong desire to see local authorities move away from directly providing services, such as housing, to a situation whereby they enable other organisations and agencies, preferably within the private sector, to supply such services. A further stated objective, that of ensuring limited public resources are targeted more effectively is also discussed. Such an objective is often taken to mean a further reduction in public expenditure.

Underlying this stated agenda, there is the Government's strong ideological dislike of public sector housing, and their desire to see choice expressed through market mechanisms. As a means of achieving this goal the Government has sought to create a so-called quasi market within the provision of rented housing, paralleling similar developments in the health and education services. Public services are now to be instilled with ethos of the market. The Government also takes the view that council housing acts to constrain economic development by restricting labour mobility.

To achieve the above objectives the Government, through the Housing (Scotland) Act 1988 (and related Great British legislation), has put in place a range of legislative mechanisms. These mechanisms are as follows: the deregulation of rents; the introduction of Tenant's Choice; the expansion of large scale voluntary transfers of public sector housing stock to other landlords; and finally the establishment of Scottish Homes, the body effectively charged with implementing these objectives.

Having examined the Government's objectives, and then discussed the mechanisms it has put in place to ensure such objectives are met, the book goes on to look at the various housing options open to tenants of public sector landlords, whether they be housed by local authorities, New Town Corporations or Scottish Homes (formerly the Scottish Special Housing Association). The options discussed are the purchase of property through the Right to Buy, and its latest variant, namely, Rent to Mortgage. Examination is also made of the prospects for tenants staying with their current public sector landlord. The mechanisms for switching to an alternative landlord, either existing or yet to be established, through the mechanisms of Tenant's Choice or voluntary transfers are also detailed.

With the latter two options in mind the book then reviews the various types of landlord available for those tenants wishing to transfer out of the public sector. These new landlords can be categorised into four groupings, namely, private landlords, private housing trusts, housing associations and housing co-operatives.

Following through the transfer process one stage further there is then a discussion of the financial realities of such a transfer option. Given that all landlords will look to Scottish Homes for some sort of financial assistance it is crucially important to understand the financial regime operated by this particular Government agency. Whether the new landlord currently exists, or is to be created out of the transfer process, it will require some level of financial assistance for both the acquisition of the houses and their subsequent improvement, if that is necessary. The amount of grant made available by Scottish Homes has clear implications for both rent levels and future tenure patterns. It is crucial that tenants' groups and professional housing workers fully understand these issues. Consideration also needs to be given to Scottish Homes' own priorities in terms of funding.

The book concludes by questioning whether the main issues in Scottish housing are being adequately addressed by this latest piece of housing legislation. It also raises questions about the true nature of choice offered to Scottish tenants. The cost of such choice is also examined, as are the related issues of accountability and democracy. Is there to be any real choice for those who rent housing in Scotland, or is it the case that choice can only be exercised at a price? Does the Government have any real commitment to public sector housing, or is their sole objective to turn as much of it as possible over to owner occupation? Can the 'independent' rented sector really be independent given its strong dependency upon the Government through its housing agency Scottish Homes? Finally, what does the future hold for those tenants who only wish to retain their secure tenancy and receive a proper service for the rent which they pay?

With the Conservatives winning a fourth consecutive General Election on the 9th April 1992, there will be little change in the broad thrust of Scottish housing policy, with a continued push to extend home ownership through the Right to Buy and Rent to Mortgage. In line with the move towards the creation of a quasi-market within the provision of public rented accommodation, attention is likely to shift towards the development of performance standards for housing management. Measurements forming part of the Citizen's Charter will also be integral to the development of competition in the provision of housing management services. These developments derive from the framework established under the Housing (Scotland) Act 1988.

2 Background

The need to improve housing conditions has been a consistent, and at times major theme in Scottish politics throughout this century. Yet the provision of a decent home for everyone still remains an aspiration which, for many, has still to be realised. The argument is often put that, because people's aspirations change, such a goal is unrealistic. Changing aspirations are, however, of little relevance to those who are presently homeless or are living in intolerable housing conditions. Dampness, disrepair, the lack of basic amenities and a lack of space all contribute to the continuing unacceptable nature of Scotland's housing conditions. If a barren, oppressive physical environment is added to this list then the scale of the problem is further enlarged. While the above issues relate to general housing conditions, those with particular housing requirements have greater difficulties, given the dearth of suitable accommodation. If a person is disabled in some way, there can be nothing worse than trying to get by in an unsuitable house. Therefore, although the severe housing shortages which dominated the post-war years have gone, solving Scotland's current housing problems requires a commitment of similar proportions, albeit that the actual solutions will have to be markedly different. Housing has, in some quarters, almost fallen off the political agenda, making it hard to generate the urgency required to tackle these issues. In order to assess the likely contribution of the Housing (Scotland) Act 1988 to Scotland's housing situation it would first be useful to outline the current state of Scottish housing. Only when a clear understanding of these problems, issues and opportunities is gained can the Government's latest piece of housing legislation be properly assessed.

SCOTTISH HOUSING UNTIL 1979

In the 19th Century the industrial revolution occurred in Scotland slightly later than in England and hence was telescoped into a shorter timescale. Large numbers of Scots moved from the rural lowlands to growing towns and cities. At the same time, many people from Ireland and the Highlands also moved to the urban centres of Scotland. This massive influx created an enormous pressure for housing which, combined with traditionally low wages, inferior housing and a small construction industry, produced slum conditions for hundreds of thousands of Scots (Morgan, 1989). By the end of the century it was widely recognised that housing in Scotland was far worse than in England (Rogers, 1989). This was equally true for the rural areas where Scotland's poorer farming industry ensured the farm labourers' cottages were of a low standard.

The 1917 Royal Commission, which examined the scale of Scotland's housing problem, concluded that the private sector was incapable of providing housing in sufficient numbers, or of an acceptable quality, to meet the demands of the working classes (HMSO, 1917). Rather than opting for a system of subsidising the landlords the Government made subsidies available to local authorities for the purpose of building and managing housing. For over half a century, from the early 1920s through to the mid 1970s, local authorities in Scotland built more houses every year than private builders. This policy was encouraged by virtually all Governments over this period. At the same time the share of housing owned by private landlords fell markedly through a combination of demolition and sales to owner occupation. Private renting is now effectively a rump in Scottish housing, representing less than six per cent of the total housing stock.

The number of council houses built fell dramatically in the late 1970s and in recent years most major local authorities have been unable to build any homes at all. Present Government policy has been to reduce the number of people renting from all public bodies, whether they be local authorities, New Town Corporations or the SSHA (now Scottish Homes). At the same time a vigorous pro-home-ownership policy has been pursued.

Since 1980 public sector tenants have had the Right to Buy their homes at significant price discounts (now standing at up to 70 per cent for a flat and 60 per cent for a house). In addition to this, all owner occupiers benefit from the generous system of mortgage interest tax relief and are exempt from capital gains tax. Related to the growth in owner occupation was the Government's strong commitment to private sector housing renovation and improvement. Since the late 1960s, housing policy has switched from demolition towards the improvement and repair of private sector housing stock.

For tenants the pattern of subsidy has altered significantly over the last decade. Direct rent subsidies to local authority tenants have been cut. By 1989-90 the average Scottish owner occupier received £750 annual subsidy from central Government, through mortgage tax relief, while direct subsidies to council tenants had fallen, on average, to £94 for that year. As a direct result of these cuts in Government subsidy, council rents have inevitably risen by approximately 200 per cent in real terms since 1979. That said, with the introduction of the Housing Benefit system in 1982, an individual subsidy system which contributed towards the rent has become an alternative means of subsidising the revenue side of public sector housing. Today some 70 per cent of Scottish tenants are in receipt of some form of Housing Benefit. The Government has made it clear for some time that it wishes to see the removal of indiscriminate subsidies, such as those on building a house, and their replacement by subsidies which focus on those in greater need.

The overall effect of housing policies since 1979 has been a substantial increase in owner occupation and a corresponding decrease in the number of people renting from the public sector agencies. At the same time the Government's renovation policies, for private sector stock, have made significant inroads into reducing the number of sub-tolerable houses in Scotland. It is, however, also the case that the overall level of disrepair, in both the public and private stock, has grown substantially over this period.

There have also been a number of other developments in Scottish housing, some long standing and others relatively new, which require the concerted efforts of Government to tackle. Although the Government would argue that its policies have addressed these issues, a lack of resources has tended to ensure these problem have persisted, or in fact got worse. It would, therefore, be useful to list these issues.

CURRENT SCOTTISH HOUSING ISSUES

The problems and issues which are of relevance within this context are homelessness, dampness and disrepair, the peripheral estates, rural housing, and the requirement for special needs accommodation. Although these issues are clearly inter-related they have certain unique aspects.

HOMELESSNESS

Homelessness is not a new problem. What is different, however, is the unprecedented rise in the numbers of homeless people. In 1981 14,868 households had to ask the local authority for help because they had nowhere to live. By 1988 this figure had risen to 24,341, an increase of 64 per cent over the period (SDD, 1989). These figures are bad enough, but it should be remembered that there are likely to be many more households who do not ask for help.

The reasons for people becoming homeless are wide and varied. A common reason is that parents, friends or relatives can no longer put them up. Young single people are most likely to become homeless in this way. The breakdown of relationships is another contributory factor. The fact that one in seven Scottish households are officially overcrowded helps add to this problem. Another growth area for homelessness is mortgage default. With owner occupation becoming more accessible to those on low incomes the possibility of default increases. According to Shelter, mortgage repossessions in Scotland have risen by a factor of three between 1980 and 1989. It was estimated that nearly 900 houses were repossessed in 1989 (Shelter, 1990). Given that these figures only refer to building society mortgages, and not those issued by the banks, the actual level of repossession is likely to be significantly higher. The recent high interest rates further compounded the problem.

As a result of a shortage in accommodation, many local authorities have had to make use of cheap hotels, the so-called Bed and Breakfast establishments. Although such solutions to homelessness are thought to be an urban phenomenon, rural authorities also make extensive use of this type of accommodation. Over the last few years their use has declined, particularly in Glasgow. Some authorities have also made use of caravans to deal with homelessness.

With council house sales reducing the available stock for rent, and new construction having almost ceased, it is hard to see how this particular issue can be adequately tackled. Public investment in rented housing has for years been insufficient to maintain the existing houses let alone build sufficient new dwellings. Present private rented sector accommodation is largely unacceptable, and in certain instances is a positive danger to the health of residents. Homelessness will only be reduced through adequate Government investment in housing. Reducing overcrowding from its current unacceptable level would be a useful start.

DAMPNESS AND DISREPAIR

In the words of the Scottish Affairs Committee in its 1984 report on dampness, *'Damp living conditions are not just a minor inconvenience for those who have to endure them - they constitute a major social evil which at its worst renders otherwise perfectly decent homes unfit for human habitation.'* (House of Commons, 1984, pxii). The problem is that thousands of people are currently expected to reside in such conditions. The Scottish Development Department (SDD) itself estimated that over one in four homes were affected by dampness. Only with the publication of the long awaited Scottish National House Condition Survey will the true extent of this problem be known. In Glasgow, where a local house condition survey was recently completed, it was revealed that 28 per cent of the city's entire housing stock was affected by dampness. Put another way, a total of 203,000 Glaswegians live in a damp house (Robertson, 1989a). There is also conclusive evidence that dampness, and particularly mould growth, can cause serious health problems for children (Hunt et al., 1988).

The physical causes of the problem revolve around inadequate heating systems, unacceptably poor standards of insulation, and a high incidence of disrepair, either by the private owner or the local authority. The level of disrepair is also an issue in itself, but again quantifying the scale of the problem awaits the National House Condition Survey.

Having focused on the physical causes of the problem there are also social explanations which relate, almost solely, to the high incidence of poverty present within Scotland. In essence dampness results from the combination of poor people living in poor quality accommodation.

It is particularly focused within the post-war peripheral housing estates and the more recently constructed system built high-rise and deck-access blocks.

PERIPHERAL ESTATES

The inadequacy of much of Scotland's housing in terms of design, layout and location is an extremely difficult issue to quantify. Much of the public housing stock, built after the war, employed non-traditional construction techniques. The massive demand for housing ensured that this option was a necessity. Through time, however, a significant proportion of these houses have required substantial up-grading. In extreme cases, such as Orlit housing, demolition has often been necessary.

Outwith this non-traditional stock a significant proportion of post war housing was poorly constructed and badly located. This, combined with the cheap building material employed, has created what are now considered unacceptable living conditions. While the internal fitments represented a marked improvement for the tenants escaping the squalor of the slums, they are totally inadequate by today's standards.

System built housing, such as high-rise and deck-access blocks, although above the tolerable standard have, in recent years, had a massive amount of attention focused upon them. Large scale clearance or complete refurbishment has taken place in most Scottish towns and cities, and such work is likely to be even more frequent in future.

The previously mentioned problems of dampness and disrepair are closely associated with all the above house types. It is also the case that Scotland's population profile is moving more towards small, often single person households, making these properties, built for families, less attractive.

The poor quality of the external environment in so many of Scotland's housing estates is another major issue. While statements, such as *forget all these fancy notions of yours about landscape or play areas or shops or open space. We've got enough to do to get people housed'* (Nuttgens, 1990) are understandable, given the post war housing problem, their persistence today is unacceptable.

Scotland has a major peripheral housing estate problem. Put at its simplest, it is that the wrong type and size of house is available in the wrong locations. Unfortunately, current solutions to this major problem are still tied to the old layouts and house type patterns. There would seem to be a financially imposed dearth of imagination in regard to future upgrading and renewal of these estates. This is a major challenge, which, given the evidence to date, will be avoided through adherence to strict and often unrealistic cost limits, which derive more from the planning powers of the accountant than the challenge of the problem at hand. As a consequence this problem will rebound on Scotland in years to come. Yet, why should it be necessary to be hidebound by the planning disasters of the past?

RURAL HOUSING

Although most Scottish people live in and around the four major cities, Scotland also possesses substantial rural districts. The problems of poor housing and poverty are just as serious in these areas as within the towns. If anything, the problems are worse given that, on average, rural incomes are ten per cent lower, while the cost of living is ten per cent higher than the rest of the country (COSLA, 1987). This often creates the impression of a unique housing problem. Although it would be wrong to say that there are unique rural housing problems, given the diversity of rural circumstances, the same housing problems have different implications and outcomes within these varied rural environments.

Rural housing issues revolve around housing supply and access, tenure mix and house conditions (Robertson and McGregor, 1987). In regard to the first of these, rural areas tend to have a significantly lower housing turnover. This is partly a reflection of the higher proportion of elderly within the community. Rural areas are also typified by a high degree of owner occupation. Due to this, the supply of housing is largely determined by the market. This creates problems for low income groups because, not only do they have to compete for housing in the local community, but the demand for second and retirement homes acts to further constrain choice.

Access to housing is largely dependent upon the income and social class characteristics of the local area. For high income groups access is relatively unconstrained. They can purchase second hand or newly built property. Access for low income groups is largely influenced by the activities of the higher income groups. Outwith the owner occupied sector alternative access is found via the public or private rented sectors. Private rental, which includes tied cottages, has declined markedly in recent years, mainly in response to the re-organisation of the agricultural economy. As the need for farm labour has declined, farm workers' houses have either been sold off to the tenants or put onto the open market. While certain properties became second homes or were retained as holiday lets, others were merely left to decay.

Public provision of council houses in rural areas is low, particularly in the remoter districts (Mackay and Laing, 1982). The severe cutbacks in housing finance since 1975 have placed a major constraint on redressing this lack of council housing. The level of council house sales in the rural districts has also created both access problems and financial difficulties for the local authorities.

Although housing tenure is largely the outcome of supply and demand it should also be considered in its own right. Tenure mix is primarily the outcome of the geographical and economic characteristics of the localities and these have political and social consequences. The diversity of rural environments, as noted earlier, is a result of these influences.

One of the biggest problems in the rural areas is the poor physical condition of so much of the housing stock. In fact, the more remote the rural district the greater the level of disrepair. The reasons for this focus upon the low wages paid to agricultural labourers and the dramatic changes in the local farming economy. Solutions to this problem have been hard to initiate given the high levels of poverty, the high costs of such work, particularly in remote districts, and the inappropriate nature of much housing legislation, in that it is largely designed to tackle the problem of disrepair within an urban context. Too often urban considerations and solutions affect the ability of rural areas to address a problem.

If the rural areas are to play a greater part in the economy of Scotland it is essential that adequate housing is provided within these communities. Unfortunately, since 1917 Government housing policies, while acknowledging the problems, have chosen to focus upon urban housing solutions.

SPECIAL NEEDS ACCOMMODATION

Special needs groups cover those people for whom physical adaptions, or the arrangement of support or care services are a necessary part of their housing to enable them to maintain independent and fulfilling lives within the community (Brailey et al, 1989). The groups which typically fall into this category are people with a mental handicap or a mental health problem, people with physical disabilities or chronic illnesses, abused women, ex-offenders; people with drug or alcohol problems, vulnerable young people and the elderly.

Special needs can often be met through the allocation of suitable mainstream housing. In fact, it can be argued that those who provide housing should only have to make suitable accommodation available to people with special needs, who then, in turn, are able to obtain the necessary care and support required from the social work and health services. As it is not always possible to obtain this type of care and support in this way, it is often considered more appropriate to develop projects which link support and housing together through various forms of supported accommodation. The Government itself is supportive of 'Care in the Community' schemes, although the finance to facilitate their expansion has not, to date, been forthcoming. Such developments are also too often tangled up within the bureaucracies of Health Boards, Social Work Departments and housing providers. It is also worth noting that the idea of 'Care in the Community' has been pursued since the early 1960s.

Demand for special needs accommodation is difficult to quantify, given the wide range of measures employed to record the size of each of these groups, or categories. There is, however, no doubt that significant demand for special needs accommodation exists throughout Scotland. Yet, until a proper commitment is given to this area, information on needs and demand will remain somewhat subjective.

Having looked at the major issues within Scottish housing, the context has been set for the subsequent discussion of the Housing (Scotland) Act 1988. This Act represents the Conservative Government's second concerted attempt at initiating radical change within Scotland's dominant housing tenure, namely council housing. The previous approach, under the Tenant's Rights etc (Scotland) Act 1980, was to introduce, and actively promote, the Right to Buy. This Act also greatly enhanced the tenant's rights in relation to their public sector landlord. The Housing (Scotland) Act 1988, with its emphasis upon expanding choice within rented housing may, therefore, represent a move away from the Government's perceived pre-occupation with the promotion of owner occupation. Only through examining the various options open to tenants, drawing out the various issues which arise, will it be possible to assess whether this particular piece of housing legislation can effectively address Scotland's housing problems.

3 Government Objectives

In the White Paper *Housing: The Government's Proposals for Scotland*
(SDD, 1987a) four key objectives are stated. These are: to encourage
the spread of home ownership; revitalise the private rented sector; assist
local authorities to become 'enablers' within the housing market, as
opposed to direct 'providers' of housing; and to target public expenditure more effectively. It would be useful to examine each of these
objectives in some detail.

ENCOURAGE THE SPREAD OF HOME OWNERSHIP

The first objective, that of further extending the spread of home
ownership, has been the cornerstone of Conservative housing policy
since the mid-1950s, if not earlier. Within the Housing (Scotland) Act
1988 there is only one amendment to the Right to Buy provisions,
namely, that the full discount available on purchasing a council house
will be available five years after its construction. Given that few, if any,
council houses have been constructed in the last decade this would not,
on the face of it, seem an important change. It does, however, ensure
that very few new council houses will be constructed in the future
because the receipt arising from their possible sale, five years on, will
be insufficient to clear the District Council's outstanding debt upon
the properties. As a result the local authority, or more accurately its
tenants, would still have to pay the outstanding debt charges upon the
house. It is also the case that major repair works carried out on council
stock, through the District Council's capital programme, would be
totally discounted after five years. This places a similar financial
burden on the Housing Revenue Account. It should, however, be
pointed out that, due to local authority accounting practices, very few
District Councils are in a position to include the major repair elements
when calculating the outstanding debt on a particular council house.
At the same time, due to the Government's tight control of District
Council housing budgets, the vast majority of local authorities are
dependent upon council house sales receipts to fund the necessary
capital repair works on their housing stock.

This minor amendment of the Right to Buy is not specifically designed to encourage the spread of home ownership but, rather, to restrict the construction of new council houses. More significantly, increased interest in the Right to Buy will be, and has been, generated from the confusion and uncertainty created within the minds of tenants as a consequence of the Government's latest piece of housing legislation (see Figure One, page 45).

The prospect of ever-increasing rents without any improvement in service is a related, but more tangible mechanism to encourage this particular form of tenure diversification. At the same time the expansion of owner occupation is the number one priority for the Government's newly established housing agency Scottish Homes. They, therefore, will be expected to produce a number of initiatives within this policy area, particularly in regard to so-called 'low cost' home ownership.

Although again not directly related to the 1988 legislation, the Government recently introduced a new home ownership scheme designed to further expand owner occupation at the cheaper end of the market. As the then Prime Minister, Margaret Thatcher stated, in announcing the scheme at the Scottish Conservative Party Conference in 1989, *"we want to try to get at people who would like to buy their homes but can't quite afford it"* (Glasgow Herald, 1989). According to Scottish Homes, who were given the task of piloting the scheme, Rent to Mortgage was designed to fill a 'market niche' just below that of the Right to Buy (Webster, 1989).

Tenants wishing to take advantage of the scheme would purchase their home at the market price, less the standard discounts available under the Right to Buy. This discount is, however, reduced by a standard 15 per cent for the specific purpose of making Rent to Mortgage less attractive than the Right to Buy. The next step is to take the tenant's current rent and add ten per cent to *'reflect the increased benefits of ownership'*. An allowance for owner occupier costs such as repairs, insurance and service charges is then deducted. The figure, for this purpose, is fixed at £5.00 per week for a house and £7.50 per week for a flat. Although the purchaser cannot be made to spend these amounts these are planned to be incentives to ensure the house is properly maintained.

The amount of money left, after these additions and deductions, is then used to calculate the maximum mortgage the tenant could afford. The mortgage would normally come from either a building society or a bank. The proportion of the discounted market price not covered by the mortgage, would become an interest free 'deferred financial commitment' that would be held by the Government's housing agency Scottish Homes. This is expressed as a fixed percentage of the market value. It would, as a result, rise or fall in line with changes in the market value. That said, the 'deferred financial commitment' is reduced each year by the additional percentage points of discount the purchaser would have accrued had they remained a tenant. There would be a ceiling on the discount, similar to the Right to Buy, less the 15 per cent. The Rent to Mortgage purchaser is free to redeem the deferred financial commitment, either in whole or in part at any time. But it has to be redeemed if and when the dwelling is sold.

The pilot scheme was only available to tenants of Scottish Homes (formerly the SSHA) and New Town tenants who opt to transfer to Scottish Homes. Although extended in April 1991 to all public sector tenants, local authorities have been reluctant to take the scheme on as it represents a financial burden on them, and more importantly reduces the opportunity for a capital receipt accruing to themselves. Rent to Mortgage is not available to those tenants who are in receipt of Housing Benefit, thus effectively limiting it to approximately 30 per cent of Scottish tenants.

The scheme is deliberately made less attractive than the Right to Buy because receipts from public sector housing sales are of crucial importance to overall levels of Public Expenditure on Scottish housing, as will be illustrated later. Although Rent to Mortgage is designed to be of interest to those wishing to take out a growing capital stake in their house, the Right to Buy is still financially far more attractive. It may also result in those who purchase on the scheme being effectively trapped in their homes, unable to move because they would have insufficient cash to buy a new house on the open market. They also have full responsibility for repairs and maintenance even although they are, in reality, but a part owner. The scheme does, however, illustrate the Government's strong commitment to reducing the overall scale of public sector housing, and its continuing reliance upon Scotland to act as a test bed for such ideas.

REVITALISE THE PRIVATE RENTED SECTOR

Conservative Governments, over the last thirty years, have had an ideological commitment to help revive the declining private rented sector. The Rent Act 1957, and the establishment of the Housing Corporation under the Housing Act 1964, provide tangible evidence of this. Such a pre-occupation has been derided by many academic commentators who have insisted that private landlordism, although dead, merely refuses to lie down (Kemp (ed), 1988). Seen in this light the latest legislative offerings fit into a long standing policy objective of Conservative politics. Accordingly, in the eyes of many, the 1988 Act has the same chance of achieving this particular objective as its predecessors (Whitehead and Kleinman, 1986; Whitehead, 1987).

To give the private sector an air of legitimacy, as well as provide a sufficient number of housing organisations to carry forward these plans, the Government has chosen to incorporate the broad housing association movement within a new private landlord categorisation. Hence the need to call this new tenure block the 'independent' rented sector.

Housing associations have always had an ambiguous tenure status which has altered depending upon which particular Government was in power at the time (Back and Hamnett, 1987). Within this context the formulation of the new 'independent' rented sector is an obvious progression. It also has the added benefit of enhancing the tarnished image of private landlordism which, in the public eye, equates too readily with Rachmanism. Within a Scottish context private landlordism throws up images of tenement squalor and exploitation.

TRANSFORM LOCAL AUTHORITIES INTO 'ENABLERS' RATHER THAN 'PROVIDERS'

The Government's third objective is to change the emphasis of the local authorities' role in relation to housing. Although the Scottish version of the White Paper is not as strongly worded as its English counterpart, in that the Government still envisages a significant role for the local authorities in the provision of rented housing, this nevertheless is to be reduced through time. As stated *'Local authorities will remain substantial landlords'* but *'the scale of provision will gradually diminish'* (SDD, 1987a, para 1.22).

In essence the Government wants local authorities to shift their role towards that of enablers, agencies identifying problems and passing them on to other relevant organisations to deal with. Four aims specifically mentioned by the Government under this heading are to involve the 'independent' rented sector and the tenants themselves in improving standards; to assist in the diversification of ownership to allow the development of more balanced and mixed communities; to ensure a good service is provided for those tenants who choose to remain within the local authority; and finally, to put more effort into a strategic role. It should be said these are a continuation of existing practice for many local authorities,. The new policy environment in which local authorities now find themselves is markedly different from the one they have recently left. In particular their ability to diversify tenure by using housing associations and co-operatives is not the same process as it once was, given the changes in both the financial and new tenure status of these organisations.

Further, local authorities question how they can become enablers when they possess limited access to the capital which is essential to facilitate such initiatives. It is likely, therefore, that the enabling function for local authorities will be very much a passive one, reacting to and facilitating the policy objectives and ambitions of others, rather than directly initiating the changes themselves.

TARGET PUBLIC EXPENDITURE MORE EFFECTIVELY

The fourth objective, that of targeting public expenditure more effectively, has been the cornerstone of all Government policy since the early 1970s. Equating this objective to facilitating an ever increasing role for private finance has, however, been a trade mark of the present Government, since coming to power in 1979.

In housing terms this objective has tended to be focused upon the promotion of owner occupation, through the variety of mechanisms previously discussed. The introduction of a large element of private finance into the work of housing associations is a relatively new departure. The provision of rented accommodation by these organisations was previously almost totally publicly funded.

Undoubtedly the idea of stretching limited public resources through accessing private sector finance seems, at first sight, attractive. If half the cost of a housing project came from private sources then it would be possible, so the argument goes, to build twice as many houses for the same level of public investment. Unfortunately, because the cost of servicing such a large private loan is considerably higher than that of previous loans covering between five and ten per cent of the cost of the project, it may not be possible for those on low incomes to live in the houses provided. Consequently, those housing organisations dependent upon Government subsidy, such as housing associations and housing co-operatives, have since 1989 been locked into an argument about the level of public subsidy required to ensure the housing produced is affordable to those they wish to house. The critical elements of this debate are the level of subsidy to be made available, the cost of private money and the combined influence of both on the resulting rent level.

What is and what is not an affordable rent is the crucial issue for debate within housing association circles. It may not be possible to resolve this question because, up to this point in time, the Government and consequently its new housing agency Scottish Homes, profess no view on what is an affordable rent. The debate, as a result, has no real focus. Such a position is fortunately not sustainable in the long term. Given the importance of the affordability debate (or non debate), this topic will be referred to more fully later.

THE BROADER POLICY FRAMEWORK

While the above represents the Government's stated housing objectives there are broader developments within Conservative policy which impinge upon housing and, to some extent, set the policy context for this legislation. It is well known, for example, that the Government over the last decade has wished to reduce the role of local authorities (Ridley, 1988; Minford et al., 1987). Council housing, to some extent represents the last major service function administered by local authorities. Previously local authorities ran the gas, electricity, public transport and a host of other services and functions. Through time their involvement in these other areas has diminished. By separating the provision of rented housing from District Councils another significant role would be lost and their position further weakened.

Council housing also reflects a form of service delivery which is much criticised by Government. It epitomises a cornerstone of the despised Welfare State and, therefore, one major component of the nation's culture of dependency (Mason, 1985; Minford et al., 1987). Choice within council housing is not exercised through the market mechanism, but through inefficient queuing, a system more in tune with the 'discredited' former regimes of the Eastern Bloc. The extension of choice through the creation of a quasi market system is, not surprisingly, the central theme running through the Government's current housing policy. In the future choice should be exercised through the market. The clear analogy of this is that those who cannot compete within this market will have limited choice.

The Government also take the view that council housing is a serious constraint upon labour mobility (Tingle, 1986). This view crops up in the White Paper where it states that council housing has *hindered Scotland's capacity to respond to economic problems and challenges'* (SDD, 1987a, para 1.2).

The privatisation of council housing, either through the expansion of council house sales or through the transfer of ownership to quasi-private landlords will, the Government hopes, instil market disciplines on to those who own, manage or rent this ex-council housing. It will also lead local authorities to re-assess their own systems and methods of managing rented accommodation. Hence, within the White Paper the Government states that,

> "*The private sector can offer greater flexibility and responsiveness to market demand. It can provide housing in a way that encourages labour mobility and meets the changing needs of individuals and the economy as a whole. Restoring an active private rented sector will allow individuals to take advantage of improved prospects in different parts of the country. It will help progress towards a better match between supply and demand for labour.*"
>
> Source: SDD, 1987a, para 1.10.

The Government's proposals for council housing, over the next decade centre around the desire for more privatisation, which goes well beyond council house sales. This privatisation strategy revolves around three main themes. In the first place, the market is seen as the best means of allocating housing resources. Secondly, the market also instils market disciplines on those who provide housing. Finally, council housing has been, but should no longer be, a constraint on labour mobility. It is within this broader policy framework that the recent changes in housing legislation have been drafted. These are examined in more detail in the next section.

4 Government Mechanisms

Having examined the Government's objectives, within the broader policy context, it is now necessary to outline the four mechanisms which have been developed to ensure these objectives are met. The four mechanisms examined are the Deregulation of Rents, Tenant's Choice, voluntary transfers and Scottish Homes. All but voluntary transfers are embodied within the Housing (Scotland) Act 1988. Amendments to the legislation covering the transfer of local authority housing stock to another landlord are part of the Housing Act 1988. Although this Act mainly deals with England and Wales, it contains sections which also cover Great Britain as a whole.

DEREGULATION OF RENTS

There is a long standing belief that the demise of the private landlord was simply due to the introduction of Rent Controls during the First World War. Rent Controls were originally designed to prevent property owners from profiteering as a result of the severe housing shortages created within the large munition production centres, such as Glasgow. Through time, the popular view was that the continuation of rent restrictions after 1919 became a hindrance to landlords making an adequate return on their investment. While this does provide a partial explanation for the demise of the private rented sector, it certainly does not provide a comprehensive answer. What is often conveniently ignored is the fact that new construction for rent effectively ceased prior to the outbreak of the First World War because better returns on investment could be made elsewhere. The political influence of landlords, who were in large part small investors, also fell away with the development of corporate capital interests (McCrone and Elliot, 1989).

Another fact which tends to be conveniently overlooked is the impact which other forms of housing provision, namely, owner-occupation and council renting, had on the market for private rented accommodation. Favourable tax treatment and subsidies helped promote owner-occupation, while through time a fluctuating system of subsidy regimes assisted the growth of council housing. No real attempt was made to extend these favourable fiscal regimes to the traditional private rented sector. Private landlordism was perceived to be too discredited, hence, no political party saw any merit in championing its revival, at least not until the late 1950s. Unfortunately, the debate surrounding the demise of the private rented sector has, for political reasons, tended to focus almost exclusively upon rent restrictions to the exclusion of everything else.

The financial attractions of owner-occupation led to a substantial, and sustained, level of sales from the private rented sector to that particular tenure (Hamnett and Randolph, 1988). In effect, the growth of owner occupation assisted greatly in the demise of private renting. Further, the development of council housing created great uncertainty within the private rented sector. Given the scale of clearance and new council house construction, especially in the late 1950s and throughout the 1960s, future prospects for private rented housing seemed somewhat limited. New council housing, after all, created competition for the private landlords even although council house rents were significantly higher than those charged by private landlords. Yet, people who had sufficient income chose to move even although costs in terms of rent, travel time and social amenity were known to be substantially more in their new council house. These facts, however, have not been lost on those promoting new forms of tenure which guarantee improvements in living conditions.

Government policy has, for its own reasons, chosen to ignore the comprehensive analysis of why the private rented sector went into almost terminal decline. For the Government it is simply a matter of rent controls. All that would be required to revitalise the private, or newly christened 'independent', rented sector is the deregulation of rents. Hence, under the Housing (Scotland) Act 1988, all new tenancies issued by these 'independent' landlords are assured.

Assured tenancies had not existed in Scotland previously. This new form of tenancy is now the standard form of tenancy outwith the council sector. It is also the case that existing Scottish Homes and New Town tenants have secure tenancies.

Under the assured tenancy the rent and terms of the tenancy are to be 'freely negotiated between landlord and tenant' (SDD, 1987a, para 4.9). Rent levels do not necessarily have to reflect the market if, for example, the landlord is in receipt of grants, or other forms of public subsidy. That said, it is clear Government wishes to see the doctrine of the market operating within rented housing. Tenants will be safeguarded, to some extent, against later unreasonable upward revisions of the agreed rent by a right under certain circumstances to go to a Rent Assessment Committee for arbitration. There will, however, be no public register of rents for assured tenancies unless the Secretary of State so decides and the rent set by the Rent Assessment Committee will be a market one, taking account of subsidy levels or tenants' ability to pay. Without such a register it will be very difficult for tenants to argue about what should be the appropriate level of rent.

Assured tenancies also reduce the statutory rights tenants receive under secure tenancies offered by the local authorities. For example, assured tenancies were originally to have no right of succession. The right of succession to a widow, or widower, was only a last-minute concession granted in the House of Lords. Although widows and widowers can now obtain succession, the statutory provision clearly bears harshly on the sons and daughters of tenants who, in effect, have no right to inherit the tenancy of what could have been their home.

There are also statutory provisions for mandatory eviction for three months' rent arrears or discretionary eviction for a history of delay in rent payments. While the secure tenancy has no mandatory grounds for eviction the new assured tenancy has eight separate grounds. Interestingly, the loss or retention of the Right to Buy is variable. All new tenancies in both housing associations and co-operatives will be assured, as will those resulting from the Tenant's Choice procedures. They will have no Right to Buy. Tenants who change their landlord through the voluntary transfer mechanism will retain this right.

As it was the Government's desire to see a greater role for private investors within rented housing it was necessary to introduce this form of tenancy. This is because private investors require to be satisfied that their investment is secured. Hence the need to have a deregulated rent and a reduction in tenants' rights over security of tenure. Rented property, as a consequence, will move back to being viewed as an asset from which a profit can be made, as opposed to being someone's home.

Seen within this context, it is clear why Assured tenancies have been introduced. It is somewhat ironic, therefore, that the Government, in its White Paper, takes the time to highlight the great strides made in improving the status and rights of tenants within the public sector, through the introduction of the Tenant's Rights etc. (Scotland) Act 1980. Under this latest piece of legislation the Government is, in effect, repealing its earlier provisions for those who choose to move into a new tenancy situation. The issue of choice is, therefore, of crucial importance. The Government may wish to argue that the loss of rights reflects the responsibility which accrues from holding a tenancy in the new 'independent' rented sector. Yet, for most tenants the differences and distinctions between their new and old landlords may not be blatantly obvious. For those tenants who are forced to accept a new landlord, due to a lack of real choice, or who have in fact been forcibly transferred against their will, this represents a major deterioration of their housing rights.

Finally, given that the decline of the private rented sector is more complex than the Government chooses to acknowledge, it is not necessarily the case that rent deregulation alone will lead to a revival of this sector. That said, given the much larger role envisaged for private investment in rented accommodation, there is likely to be greater insecurity for tenants in the future, particularly for those on low incomes.

TENANT'S CHOICE

The Housing (Scotland) Act 1988 confers on tenants a new right, that of transferring their tenancy to another landlord of their choice, either on an individual or collective basis. Tenant's Choice is an individual right, unlike the situation in England and Wales. As a result even tenants in blocks of flats have an individual right to transfer. This new right is seen as being a means of allowing tenants to exercise real choice in rented housing. Within this context it fits well with the underlying Government philosophy outlined earlier. Yet for real choice to exist, there needs to be a range of options on offer and, secondly, there should also be the chance to exercise further choices should the initial option prove unsatisfactory.

Under both these criteria Tenant's Choice fails for it is a once only move out of the public sector, and there are presently a restricted number of landlord choices available to tenants. Landlords specifically mentioned in the White Paper for transfer purposes are housing associations, housing co-operatives and private landlords. Public sector landlords are excluded from these new arrangements. Given the Government's strong emphasis upon improving choice in housing, such a restriction merely reflects political dogmatism. For tenants of the Scottish New Towns, who previously understood they would be transferring to the local authority after the New Town Corporation was wound up, this restriction creates much uncertainty.

Scottish Homes, the Government's new housing agency, has a role to play in the Tenant's Choice arrangements. Not only does it have the power to act as 'matchmaker', between tenants and new landlords, but it also has the power to approve Tenant's Choice landlords *'on the basis of their suitability and viability'* (SDD, 1987a, para 6.10). It can also issue a general approval to *'all persons of a particular description'* (HMSO, 1988a, clause 57). An amendment passed in the House of Commons, one of only very few, also allows Scottish Homes to approve transfers subject to particular conditions. While this is clearly a double edged sword it could prove a useful mechanism for tenants' groups, in that they could insist upon certain safeguards being incorporated into a transfer, in the event of, for example, a landlord proving unsuitable or alternatively going into liquidation. At present if either situation arose the landlord's approved status could be revoked. Yet tenants who had already transferred would be left, either at the mercy of the receivers or, alternatively would still continue to be managed by a landlord who had been found to be unsatisfactory. As a means of addressing such criticism the Government has said the approval process will *'aim to ensure that the new landlords are financially stable and capable of managing their homes to a high standard while giving value for money'* (SDD, 1988b).

The price and conditions of the transfer are detailed in the Housing (Scotland) Act 1988, clauses 56 to 64. Broadly the Act states that the new landlord will have to pay the market value, subject to tenancy, which is usually between 25 and 33 per cent of the vacant possession value. The new landlord will have the right of access to information for the purposes of survey and valuation. While this is normal practice in any transfer of stock from District Councils to another landlord there are two further instructions to the District Valuer which place this form of transfer into a new valuation category.

In the first place, under clause 58(7)(d) of the Act, it is stated that the price of transfer should also have to take into account the *'cost of such works as are reasonably necessary to put the house into the state of repair required by the landlord's repairing obligations*. In certain instances, where a property was in a particularly poor state of repair, it could require the existing landlord to make a payment to the new landlord. The tenants that remain with the District Council would ultimately foot this bill through their rents.

The absurdity of this valuation practice is best illustrated by using the example of an individual purchasing a second hand car. A car is offered for sale at its going market value, namely £1,500. The prospective purchaser, estimating that £800 would be required for mechanical and body work repairs, therefore offers £700 to purchase the car, an offer which the seller must accept. Yet market value should, and, in all other valuation situations, does reflect the condition of the item for sale. Why should disrepair in this particular valuation context be double counted? (First on the basis of its market value and second in regard to the works that may require to be carried out.) This must be solely to ensure that the asset base provided by the District Council's housing stock is utilized to subsidise the activities of these new landlords. Such landlords would also, as a result, not necessarily look for substantial Government subsidies for any subsequent refurbishment work.

The second instruction to the District Valuer, which could act to further reduce the price paid by the new landlord, is that they have to assume there are no buyers except persons previously approved by Scottish Homes (HMSO, 1988b, clause 53(8)(7)). Again using the analogy of an everyday purchase this represents the equivalent of going into a shop to purchase a coat and stating that, as the only customer approved to purchase the coat, you will only pay £25, rather than the £150 marked on the price tag.

By lowering the acquisition price to the new landlord, the total cost of both acquiring and modernising the property, if such work was required, can be substantially reduced in two ways. In the first place the cost of acquisition and modernisation is lowered. Secondly, this cost reduction can result in a greater proportion of the cost of such work being carried by a private loan. Using the District Council's asset base to enhance the role for private investment is, in fiscal terms, a useful device to benefit the Treasury. There is, however, a cost to pay, and that cost is borne by those tenants who remain with the local authority.

VOLUNTARY TRANSFERS
Tenant's Choice, given what was said earlier, would seem to have a limited role to play in the transfer of publicly owned housing stock to alternative landlords. The Government, perhaps realising this, chose, under the Housing Act 1988, to amend the procedures for the voluntary transfer of housing stock from a local authority (or other public body) to alternative tenures. If tenure transfers are to take place this will undoubtedly be the most commonly used mechanism.

Local authorities have always had the power to sell land, a broad definition which also includes housing stock. This power was conferred upon Scottish local authorities under the Local Government (Scotland) Act 1973. This insisted that if housing stock was sold, it would have to be at the market value. The only exemption to these provisions was if the property was deemed to be unlettable. Under the provisions of the 1973 Act the Secretary of State's permission had to be sought before any transfer could take place. Justification for this change was that housing stock held under the Housing Revenue Account could still have an outstanding public debt, for which the Government was ultimately responsibility.

Over the years these powers of transfer have been used quite extensively. In the case of local authorities transferring stock for the refurbishment and subsequent sale by the private sector an early example was provided by Martello Court in Edinburgh. This was later followed by the sale of different parts of West Pilton to a consortium of private developers. In Glasgow sales to the private sector have occurred in South Rogerfield, Easterhouse, Pendeen in Barlanark and in Priesthill. Other local authorities throughout Scotland have also been involved in this type of activity.

Larger scale transfers to newly formed community based housing organisations, such as co-ops and housing associations, have been relatively recent developments, with Glasgow to some extent leading the way. Transfers of this type have occurred in the Priesthill, Broomhouse, Calvay, Possil, Southdeen and Ballantay districts of the city. Similar transfers have also occurred in Niddrie House in Edinburgh, Hunters Crescent in Perth, Long Park in Kilmarnock, Ferguslie Park in Paisley, Trafalgar in Clydebank and in Whitfield in Dundee. A number of similar transfers are presently being negotiated throughout Scotland.

Under the Housing Act 1988 a transfer can now only take place if the Secretary of State is satisfied that a due level of consultation, with the existing tenants, has taken place and that the majority do not oppose the transfer. The intention here is to give the tenants themselves a greater say in the transfer process, and to some extent act as initiators of the process. That said, the Housing Act 1988 and the subsequent Government paper on voluntary transfers (SDD, 1988b) imply that much of the necessary initiative, for any transfer, still lies with the local authorities themselves.

There has been much talk about the issue of ballots within the context of voluntary transfers. Undoubtedly, experiences in England and Wales, and in particular the ballot fiasco at Torbay, have acted to distort the issue (Bright, 1989). In Torbay, although the tenants voted decisively against a transfer, attempts were made to proceed on the basis that the 42 per cent who abstained should be counted as being in favour. This transfer was later abandoned.

The only tenants who have been given an automatic right to a ballot, in regard to any proposed transfer, are the tenants of what was previously the SSHA. The Secretary of State made it clear that transfers of this stock will only take place if the majority of those eligible to vote support the proposed transfer, eligibility to vote being defined on the basis of tenancy. Only those with a tenancy will therefore have the right to a vote. Potentially this disenfranchises a substantial number of people who reside within the housing stock, but do not hold a tenancy. Opting for those with a tenancy is, however, regarded as the only legally acceptable, and practical, method of conducting such ballots. It should also be borne in mind that housing which is empty at the time of the ballot is excluded from the count. While this may be an obvious point to make, there are certain estates where vacant stock could well outnumber occupied houses.

The commitment to operate ballots within Scottish Homes' own stock was only achieved following public disquiet surrounding rumours about proposed stock transfers and the possibility of management 'buy-outs' during the last days of the SSHA's existence. Given this climate the Secretary of State acted to allay tenants' fears by guaranteeing that no stock transfers would take place without a ballot of those affected to ascertain their views. The Secretary of State did not, however, take the opportunity to extend such an arrangement to tenants of either District Councils or the New Town Corporations. It is also the case that this arrangement is not a legal right as it is not enshrined in statute.

For all tenants, except those who rent from Scottish Homes, there is no automatic right to a ballot. As noted earlier, the legislation merely states that the Secretary of State should be satisfied that a due level of consultation has taken place and that the majority of those affected by the transfer proposal do not oppose it. If the Secretary of State is not satisfied he is legally bound to refuse the transfer (see HMSO, 1988a, Schedule 16). The responsibility for ensuring that this due level of consultation is achieved lies solely with the District Council or New Town Corporation.

Glasgow District Council, which to some extent pioneered the establishment of the housing co-operative movement, has issued a code of conduct on transfers (GDC, 1990). In this document there is a clear commitment given to operating ballots. Only after a clear majority of those eligible to vote support a transfer proposal would the District Council consent to the disposal of stock. Final approval, however, still lies with the Secretary of State.

This procedure was to some extent a direct response to the much criticised transfer of 1,000 houses in the Windlaw district of Castlemilk from Glasgow District Council to the SSHA (TPAS, 1988). The decision to transfer this housing stock came from a vote at the end of an open public meeting, to which any member of the public could have gained entry. The disquiet this decision generated, particularly amongst the city's tenants' groups, resulted in a tightening up of transfer procedures. The meeting also served to illustrate the strong desire amongst many tenants for a marked improvement in their current living conditions. If, to achieve this improvement, it is necessary to transfer landlord then this may be a price many are willing to pay. With the leader of Glasgow District Council making it clear to the meeting that the Council could give no guarantees about future improvements the options available to the tenants were clearly narrowed.

Other local authorities who have adopted a similar code of conduct are Dundee, Edinburgh, Dumbarton and Stirling District Councils. COSLA, the representative body for local authorities in Scotland, has also encouraged its members to adopt clear policies in relation to stock transfers. The Scottish Federation of Housing Associations, the representative body of the housing association and co-operative movement in Scotland, has also issued a code of practice to its members on the subject of voluntary transfers (SFHA,1989). This clearly states that member associations will only consent to being involved in a stock transfer, from public sector stock, if there is a properly conducted ballot. Again housing association involvement will only be guaranteed if there is a significant majority of those voting in favour of the transfer. The SFHA also states that its members should not be involved in canvassing to initiate transfers, but only become involved if both tenants and local authority invite them to do so. The SFHA is currently examining its policy position in relation to the transfer of Scottish Homes stock. Therefore, although not enshrined in the legislation, it is likely that ballots will become part of any transfer process. With the principle of ballots largely accepted there is a range of other issues which arise such as information and consultation on the available options.

The legislation is unfortunately silent on what information should be available to tenants affected by a transfer proposal. It is worth noting that a number of amendments, laying down rules on the provision of information were tabled in the House of Commons. The Government chose, however, to ignore them. It has nonetheless, issued guidance on the topic prior to the enactment of the legislation in the 1988 information paper (SDD, 1988b).

As a result of the actions of Scottish Homes, the SFHA and a number of local authorities, certain safeguards in the transfer process have now been introduced. It should, however, not be forgotten that in any transfer a minority of tenants, and in certain instances a substantial minority, will be transferred against their wishes. This has been publicly acknowledged by the Scottish Office Minister, Lord James Douglas-Hamilton. All those transferring automatically move on to an assured tenancy, with the consequent loss of security of tenure. While such a change has been accepted by those who agree to transfer, those who oppose transfer will have this change imposed on them.

Tenants do not have a contractual right to a secure tenancy. Instead they have a statutory right to one. As a result their rights are enshrined in statue rather than being in the contract between tenant and local authority. Local authorities, like any other landlord, are free to sell their stock subject to the consent of the Secretary of State where appropriate. If this changes the statutory form of tenancy the local authorities' attitude, legally, is 'so be it'. The tenants can, therefore, either accept this change, join with others to oppose it, ask the local authority for another tenancy or exercise their Right to Buy. Clearly, the latter option will be outwith the financial means of many tenants so affected.

Individually, tenants have no legal right to prevent the local authority selling any of its stock just in the same way as private landlords have no restrictions placed upon them in this matter. That said, under the voluntary transfer procedures, as outlined in Schedule 16 of the Housing Act 1988 (HMSO, 1988a), tenants collectively have the legal right to stop a transfer. The Secretary of State cannot legally sanction a transfer if he is of the opinion that the majority of tenants affected are opposed to it.

In the past, District Councils such as Glasgow often got around the difficulty of unwilling participants in a stock transfer by giving them enhanced points so they could find alternative accommodation elsewhere within the council stock (Sim and Brooke, 1984). Given the scale of expected future transfers Glasgow District Council has stated it will not continue this practice. The only exception they give is in the case of tenants wishing to establish a fully mutual co-operative through the transfer process. This is because such an organisation legally requires that all members are tenants and all tenants are members. Without this transfer option such co-ops could, potentially, not be in a position to form. That said, there is the issue of whether it is correct to encourage someone to leave their home just because their neighbours wish to form a housing organisation which they do not favour.

As with Tenant's Choice the cost of the transfer is calculated on the basis of tenanted value. There are not, however, the same double discounting procedures that exist with Tenant's Choice. Yet, because the new 'independent' landlords will be looking to Scottish Homes for funding to cover both the acquisition and any subsequent modernisation work required, the funding body will have some influence upon the price paid. Further, due to the fact that the Right to Buy will be retained, in the case of voluntary transfers, the price set by the District Valuer should reflect this. The Government obviously takes the view that any private sector investment in these new landlord organisations requires a certain degree of financial protection.

This protection is in the form of further discounting the actual sale price received by the District Council. Valuation difficulties delayed the establishment of the Niddrie House Co-op in Edinburgh and held up large scale transfers in the Wester Hailes district of that city.

SCOTTISH HOMES

The final mechanism that completes the package introduced under the Housing (Scotland) Act 1988 was the establishment of Scottish Homes. This new housing agency was formed by amalgamating the Housing Corporation in Scotland, the Government body which funded and monitored Scotland's 200 housing associations, and the SSHA, the long established Government housing agency (SDD, 1987a). The merger of a direct provider of rented housing with an enabling body was considered by many to be problematic, in that the roles and functions are very different. It was also felt that it would lead to confusion, on the part of SSHA tenants, who would see one part of the organisation actively trying to dispose of their homes, a process in which other members of the same body offer them assistance in finding, or forming new landlords. The Government, however, choose to ignore these concerns, as its prime aim was to get rid of one of its two Scottish housing agencies through merging it with the other. Masking the true extent of the SSHA's massive debt was also a prime consideration (Robertson, 1989b).

To view Scottish Homes merely as a merger of these two former housing agencies would, however, be a mistake. Scottish Homes is very much a new housing organisation with a clear remit to administer the provisions of the 1988 legislation. For example, neither the Housing Corporation, nor the SSHA, had as part of their objectives the expansion of home ownership; the revitalisation of the private rented sector; encouraging local authorities to become enablers rather than direct providers of housing; or to make the best use of public resources via the introduction of private finance to fund rented housing. It is also the case that neither organisation had direct access to the comprehensive set of powers available to Scottish Homes. Perhaps a more accurate description of this organisation would be that it is an interventionist agency with a privatising purpose, very much a product of the Thatcher era.

In common with its predecessors, Scottish Homes is a quango. Quango is the abbreviation for quasi autonomous non governmental organisation. At its simplest this means that the Secretary of State for Scotland nominates all those who serve on its Board of Management. This arrangement is not something new, in that the Secretary of State appoints a total of 2,500 individuals to a number of public bodies throughout Scotland. These include Scottish Enterprise and its related Enterprise companies, the seven Health Boards, the five New Town Development Corporations, the Crofters Commission, the Countryside Commission, the Forestry Commission and a host of others. While each Scottish Homes board member receives a payment for their time, the Chairman and Deputy Chairman are both salaried.

The Chairman of Scottish Homes is Sir James Mellon, previously a career diplomat while his depute John Richards is a professional architect. The remaining board members are Tom Begg (previously a board member of the SSHA and a lecturer at Queen Margaret College, Edinburgh); Norman Lessels (partner in Chiene and Tait, Chartered Accountants); Frances McCall (founder member of Calvay Housing Cooperative); Professor Duncan Maclennan (Director of the Centre for Housing Research, University of Glasgow); and Heather Sheerin (businesswomen and committee member of Albyn Housing Society). Charles Snedden (previously board member of the SSHA and until recently Labour Convenor of Central Regional Council) was replaced by Cameron Parker (managing director of Lithgow's Ltd) following the completion of his term of appointment.. Michael Ancram, (an advocate and former Scottish Office Minister with responsibility for housing) resigned following his success in securing the Conservative Party's nomination for the parliamentary constituency of Devises. He was replaced by Daphne Sleigh, the Conservative housing spokesperson on Edinburgh District Council.

The original Chief Executive of Scottish Homes, George Irvine, came with a financial management background from Magnet Southerns, the large DIY suppliers. After completing just over two years of his five-year contract, he resigned and returned to his previous area of employment. Iain Penman, a senior civil servant was transferred from the Scottish Office to act as an interim Chief Executive, pending the filling of this post. Peter McKinlay, who also has a Civil Service background, previously as head of the Scottish Prisons Service, was appointed in January 1992. He did however have some involvement in the drafting of the Housing (Scotland) Act 1974 which refined home improvement legislation for Scotland.

Scottish Homes originally described itself as a highly decentralised organisation with day-to-day operations being conducted through thirteen District Offices. These offices worked under four regional directors who in turn reported to Scottish Homes headquarters in Edinburgh. The headquarters operation oversaw the work of the four regions and thirteen districts.

Following the ongoing structural review three trends are clear. In the first place, Scottish Homes has abolished the regional tier within its operations. This had been much criticised in that it created four separate fiefdoms which were a filter on policy for their own area leading to varying developments in different parts of the country. As a consequence there has been a marked expansion in the policy formulation remit at the centre. This reflects the realisation that a policy vacuum existed in the original structure. The second shift has been the recognition that different areas have different needs, so the functioning of the seven remaining district offices, cut from thirteen, is likely to reflect such diversity. Thirdly, the move to integrate the housing management functions with that of enabling has been abandoned. To some extent the SSHA has been recreated under the new structure, something that was argued for in 1988.

To assist Scottish Homes in meeting its objectives the Government set an original budget, for financial year 1989-90 of £193 million. In addition it also received a further allocation of £77 million to manage the ex-SSHA housing stock. The overall budget for the following year was increased slightly, to £307 million, which given the influence of inflation represented a slight cut. It should also be noted that this figure was also dependent upon receiving £110 million in receipts, the vast majority of which come from sales of ex-SSHA houses. When this level of sales was not achieved, with only just over £70 million of receipts being received, the actual Scottish Homes' programme differed markedly from that envisaged at the start of the financial year, as Table One illustrates. By far the biggest loss was the Traditional Rented programme which received nearly £12 million less than planned. Similar problems are envisaged for financial year 1991-92, although outturn figures for that year are not yet available.

In its first year of operation Scottish Homes' programme of expenditure was largely determined by the commitments it had given under its original component parts, namely the Housing Corporation and the SSHA. Housing associations involved in both renewal work and the provision of special needs accommodation, therefore, received the bulk of the enabling funding. In addition a total of £16 million was made available for Low Cost Home Ownership initiatives; £13 million for Community Ownership which covers housing association and co-op development in ex-council housing stock; £9 million was for the four Partnership areas, (namely Castlemilk in Glasgow, Ferguslie Park in Paisley, Wester Hailes in Edinburgh, and Whitfield in Dundee) and finally £7 million for Scottish Homes New Powers. Under this heading Scottish Homes can provide 'leg up' funding to private sector builders as well as issue repair, improvement and environmental improvement grants on the same basis as a local authority.

TABLE ONE

SCOTTISH HOMES APPROVED DEVELOPMENT PROGRAMME
Financial Years 1989-90 to 1992-93   *(in £ millions)*

Category	1989-90 *	1990-91 **	1990-91 +	1991-92 ++	1992/93 +++
Partnership	9.4	14.6	13.7	18.0	26.8
LCHO	15.5	20.0	16.9	17.7	20.8
Comm. Own.	13.7	19.7	14.1	21.5	39.3
New Powers	7.0	23.1	15.0	23.8	26.2
Traditional	148.0	154.0	140.1	149.3	139.2
Own Stock					
(capital)	55.2	52.2	N/A	N/A	N/A
(revenue)	22.2	23.6	N/A	N/A	N/A

* Based on programme, not outturn figures.

** Programme figures, based on the assumption that Scottish Homes would receive £110m in receipts from sales of ex-SSHA housing stock.

+ Based on outturn figures.

++ Programme figures, based on the assumption that Scottish Homes will receive £80m in receipts from sales of ex-SSHA housing stock.

+++ Programme figures, based on the assumption that Scottish Homes will receive £60m in receipts from sales of ex-SSHA housing stock.

Under the programme for 1990-91 Scottish Homes, in consultation with the Scottish Office, set out new priorities. The number one priority, as laid out in *Scottish Homes' Strategic Investment Plan* (Scottish Homes, 1989), were the four Partnership Areas. These areas were to receive a 55 per cent increase in funding for financial year 1990-91. Secondly, Scottish Homes wanted to see a significant expansion in home ownership initiatives. As a result, Low Cost Home Ownership projects received a 16 per cent increase in programmed funding. This was clearly in line with the objectives laid out in the Governments White Paper on housing.

The third priority, the expansion of Community Ownership, achieved an 18 per cent increase. The fourth area of growth, New Powers, which covered environmental improvements, local labour market initiatives but, more importantly, grant aid to private builders increased by 129 per cent. The bulk of this money was to go to private builders through the new GRO Grant system for the provision of low cost home ownership initiatives. GRO Grants are available to private companies who wish grant assistance in the provision of housing for renting and owner occupation. It is interesting that although the Government is strongly opposed to 'bricks and mortar' subsidies for the public sector, it is not reluctant to provide such subsidies for the provision of owner occupation by the private sector.

Both urban renewal and the provision of special needs accommodation, now classed together under the new heading of the Traditional Rented Programme, received only a slight increase of five per cent. Given the level of inflation, then standing at 10 per cent, this represented a cut in real terms. The Traditional Rented programme was classed as category five. The final priority for Scottish Homes, if it can be called such, is their own housing stock.

With the lack of receipts income the true nature of Scottish Homes programme differed from that planned. The biggest losers in this, as noted earlier, was the so-called Traditional Rented Programme which had to contend with an eight per cent cut. That said, all other parts of the 1990-91 programme had to be cut back, as Table One illustrates. With the Government setting Scottish Homes a figure for receipts income, and the organisation itself unable to win the argument for increased funding, the prospects for major developments and initiatives are extremely limited. The Scottish Public Expenditure figures (Scottish Office, 1990) provided advance warning of this situation (see Table Three, page 92). Hence, the Scottish Homes' programme is best described as "taking from Peter to pay Paul", with the biggest losers in this being the existing housing associations. Evidence of this trend is seen by the cut in the Traditional Rented Programme announced for financial years 1991-92 and 1992-93. Given the clear lack of funding, many new projects particularly in the peripheral estates will be of a much poorer standard to ensure the available money is stretched further. There will also be more pressure to increase private investment in the programme, even although this is likely to produce housing for owner occupation rather than rent.

Although at this point in time the Traditional Rented Programme still accounts for the bulk of Scottish Homes enabling funding it is also destined to decline in the years to come given the new set of priorities (Robertson, 1990). This is illustrated only too clearly by comparing the changes in expenditure apportioned to the different programme categories in Table One. This does, of course, raise major policy questions. Is it equitable, for example, that the four Partnership Areas, which comprise four peripheral housing estates, spend just 30 per cent less than the total Community Ownership programme for Scotland. Further, will the expansion of these two programmes cater for the various special needs groups, given that the Traditional Rented Programme is set to decline to allow this expansion?

These investment priorities also highlight the precarious position of Scottish Homes' own stock. Given the importance of raising sales receipts Scottish Homes must sell substantial numbers of its own stock, either through the Right to Buy or large scale transfers to other landlords in the 'independent' sector. These receipts represent between one quarter and a third of Scottish Homes income. Neither the Housing Corporation nor the SSHA had to operate in such a financial environment. In Scottish Homes *Strategic Investment Plan* (Scottish Homes, 1989) there is the expectation that by 1994 only 44,000 properties will be left in its management, from a total of 74,000 in 1990.

The Government, in the original consultation document *Scottish Homes* (SDD, 1987a), published in May 1987, envisaged the new organisation as being an 'enabling and funding body', with its landlord role being viewed as 'transitional'. However in the White Paper (SDD,

1987b) the Government, at least on paper, underwent a rethink. Scottish Homes would remain a major landlord, taking over not only the SSHA stock, but also other public sector stock in order to improve the houses and their standard of management. The aforementioned transfer in Windlaw in Castlemilk could be cited as evidence of this approach. Tenants of the landlord section would however be encouraged to take up different management or ownership arrangements. This slight change of presentation was the result of the high level of disquiet felt by SSHA tenants when they realised that, potentially, they could be transferred to other landlords against their will. The rumours about new management arrangements and management 'buy-outs' in the first quarter of 1989, did little to allay such fears. From what is outlined in *Scottish Homes' Strategic Investment Plan* the original course of action is now being pursued with vigour.

It is also worth pointing out, within this context, that the Government through these sales receipts is able to reduce the amount of public expenditure it commits to Scottish housing. Broadly speaking, a third of Scottish Homes annual income is expected to come from utilizing the sales receipts received from the ex-SSHA stock. This method of funding is not unique, it being common within the council house sector for many years. The difference here is that local authority sales receipts are used to fund modernisation work on their own stock. It does not finance the housing activities of other housing organisations.

Scottish Homes also inherits the SSHA's debt of approximately £760 million, half of which is at a high rate of interest, at or above 12.5 per cent. The financial strain of servicing this debt was not helped in the past by the SSHA's aggressive sales policy. With more than 20 per cent of its stock sold through the Right to Buy, its ability to pool rents was severely constrained, with fewer and fewer tenants servicing what was, proportionally, a larger debt. In response to this the Government annually provided a subsidy to balance the books, which represented the equivalent of a quarter of the SSHA's income. While the impending financial crisis gave impetus to moves to include the SSHA within Scottish Homes, exactly what impact the inheritance of this debt will have on the new organisation is something to look out for.

5   What Will Tenants Face?

For council tenants, including those with Scottish Homes (formerly the SSHA) and the New Town Corporations, the new legislation provides them with a number of 'choices' as to the future management of their homes. All the above tenants currently retain their Right to Buy, and now have the option to use the Tenant's Choice mechanism. Collectively tenants could make use of the voluntary transfer provisions. However, although council tenants can opt to stay with their present landlord the position for New Town tenants is more confused, given the Government's decision to wind up the New Town Development Corporations. Tenants of Scottish Homes have been given the assurance that they will be fully consulted on any proposals to transfer them to another landlord. It has also been stated that no Scottish Homes tenant will be transferred against their will. That said, given that the Government's initial intention was to run down its landlord responsibilities, and Scottish Homes financial dependency upon the sales receipts from ex-SSHA stock, these tenants also face a great deal of uncertainty in the near future. In this section each of the four options facing tenants will be explored in some detail.

BUY YOUR HOUSE

Given the Government's strong preference for, and commitment to, owner occupation this is undoubtedly the favoured option. Although the Government has not further enhanced the provisions of the Right to Buy, the uncertainty their proposals have generated amongst tenants has acted to expand the level of council house sales. Between 1982 and 1987 council house sales averaged 11,000 per annum. In financial year 1988-89 this figure rose to 22,668, rising in the following year to a record 29,155 (SDD, 1990). This jump in sales is also reflected more dramatically within both the SSHA and the New Town Corporations (see Figure One).

For those tenants who are young and in steady employment, the option of purchasing their home has undoubtedly become far more attractive in recent years given ever increasing rent rises. Tenants who are entitled to the full discount (60 per cent for houses and 70 per cent for flats) could now find that mortgage and insurance payments would be less than their rent.

For this group, therefore, such a switch in tenure can make financial sense. However, there are other financial considerations which tenants should take into account before purchasing their home. In the first place the repayment figures for a mortgage are not normally fixed. Mortgage repayments, and in particular the interest rate, tend to mirror closely the rate of inflation. Over the last few years this has increased quite substantially. For those on a tight budget such an increase could result in them being unable to meet their mortgage repayments. In such circumstances they could be forced to sell their home. In part reflecting this trend, house repossessions due to mortgage default, have increased in Scotland by 300 per cent between 1980 and 1989 (Shelter, 1990). As was noted earlier this increase only covers mortgages issued by building societies. It does not cover those held by banks so this rise is likely to be an underestimate.

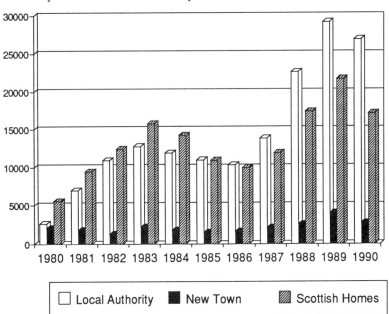

Figure One: Public Sector House Sales 1980-1990
Source: Scottish Office, 1992, table 7

Home ownership also brings with it other expenses. The first, and most obvious of these is the payment of an insurance policy to cover both building insurance and mortgage protection, or in some instances loan repayments. Secondly, all repair works to the house, either internal or external, become the owner's responsibility. If the house is within a block factored by the District Council, works may still be carried out by them, but the owner occupiers will be billed directly. The cost of day-to-day repairs, as well as any major works, such as window replacements or roof repairs, are obviously very variable and hard to predict.

It is, however, worth noting that the worst maintained housing stock, in a recent survey conducted by Glasgow District Council, was that controlled by private landlords, followed by owner occupiers (GDC, 1987). Overall, the District Council owned stock was the best maintained. These results were replicated in similar studies conducted by Nithsdale and Clackmannan District Councils.

Another financial argument that should be borne in mind in relation to council house sales is the cost of purchase against the properties' likely resale value. In certain instances building societies may refuse to provide a mortgage on the property in question because they do not consider it to have an adequate resale value given either its type or location. Orlit Housing provides a good example of building society 'red lining', as does their reluctance to fund purchases in particular housing estates. In such cases, the local authority (or other public agency) will provide a mortgage of last resort. While this may allow the tenant to purchase the property, they could well find themselves in financial difficulties should they choose to move from that property as the selling price may not necessarily cover the loan. If this happens the owner could be out of pocket by a few thousand pounds. For those who have no intention of moving this will obviously not pose a problem. But in the future, it may cause difficulties to either the heirs or executors of their estate.

For a substantial number of tenants, if not the majority, there is no possibility of them purchasing their homes. This is because they do not have secure incomes, are in receipt of some form of benefit, or are too elderly. There is also a substantial number of people who have no desire to purchase a house. For those who cannot, and those who choose not to purchase, renting is the only option.

STAY WITH THE COUNCIL
The substantial reduction in public expenditure on the provision of council housing is well documented (Maclennan and Kearns, 1989). It is, however, important to distinguish between public expenditure on capital works, which covers new house construction and modernisation, and the public subsidisation of council house revenue costs. The latter encompasses financial support for the management of council housing.

As far as the capital side of housing is concerned, indexed expenditure (in other words equalising for inflation) in 1977-78 was broadly similar to that achieved in 1987-88. In the intervening ten years, however, there was a cycle of spend which rose at the time of the 1983 and 1987 General Elections but fell sharply in the years between (Maclennan, 1989). If capital spend on council housing in 1977-78 is compared to that of 1986-87, for example, a 20 per cent fall would have been recorded. The overall trend in the decade from 1977-78 has been one of decline.

In discussing this topic it should also be borne in mind that the capital side of council housing is funded via borrowing, which is paid back through the rents. Government gives local authorities consent to borrow; they do not provide this money themselves in the form of grants. The Government, because it has to guarantee these loans, counts such expenditure as public expenditure.

A second point worth making is that in financial year 1977-78 the capital figure for council housing was composed totally of borrowing. By 1987-88 sales receipts from council house sales accounted for 30 per cent of the gross capital programme (Maclennan, 1989). In other words, the recycling of this money had effectively reduced public expenditure commitments by a third.

The Government would, however, also point out that the recycling of sales receipts benefits local authorities because they do not require to take out fresh borrowing. Local authorities often respond to this argument by questioning what other business would sell its assets, on average, for a third of their market value. Overall while real expenditure over the last decade has declined, public expenditure has been even less, thanks to the use of council house sales receipts. On the revenue side the picture is far clearer.

In its White Paper, *Housing: The Government's proposals for Scotland* (SDD, 1987b) the Government states that it will continue to reduce 'indiscriminate current expenditure subsidies' (namely Housing Support Grant and Rate Fund Contributions) (SDD, 1987b, para 6.8). Rate Fund Contributions, the money that District Councils could take from the rates to subsidise council housing, has almost been extinguished. With the introduction of the Community Charge to replace rates, such contributions are now referred to as General Fund contributions. Housing Support Grant, money that Government allocates to assist local authorities fund council housing, has seen substantial reductions over the last ten years (see Figure Two). Almost all local authorities in Scotland are now almost solely dependent upon rental income to run their housing service.

Subsidy is, however, available in the rents through the Housing Benefit system. Under the Government's accountancy practices Housing Benefit is not counted as a housing subsidy but as part of the DSS budget. The switching of subsidy away from the provision of council housing in the form of 'bricks and mortar', towards an individual form of subsidy has been a long-standing ambition of the Government. Subsidy, so the argument goes, should be directed to those in greatest need through the Housing Benefit System and not through the subsidisation of council housing construction. That said, the level of subsidy provided to Scottish council housing in this way does not compare well with the level of subsidy allowed, in the form of tax relief, for owner occupiers. Mortgage interest tax relief, for financial year 1989-90 amounted to £450 million (Hansard, 15 March 1990). Net public expenditure on council housing, in the same financial year, amounted to £475 million (Scottish Office, 1990). The Government does, however, state that it will continue to make Exchequer subsidy available on the basis of ensuring that councils achieve the proper balance between the reasonable cost of providing, maintaining and managing the housing stock and charging affordable rents.

Given what has been said earlier about the overall reduction in funds going into council housing, it is clear the Government does not envisage an expansion of its current level of support for this tenure. If anything, the above statement about Exchequer subsidies is likely to result in further cuts taking place. The Scottish Office's recently published budget report *Public Expenditure to 1992-93; A Commentary on Scottish Programme* bears this out (Scottish Office, 1990). As a result it is likely that council tenants will be paying higher rents for a declining quality of service. Add to that the financial impact on the HRA of both council house sales and stock transfers, either through Tenant's Choice or large scale voluntary transfers, then the financial burden on these tenants who remain with the local authorities will increase. In effect, unless measures are taken to pay back the outstanding debt on these properties, fewer and fewer tenants will be servicing a debt which will become proportionately larger through time. Given the lack of Government subsidies, rent levels will undoubtedly rise, encouraging more and more people to opt out of council housing.

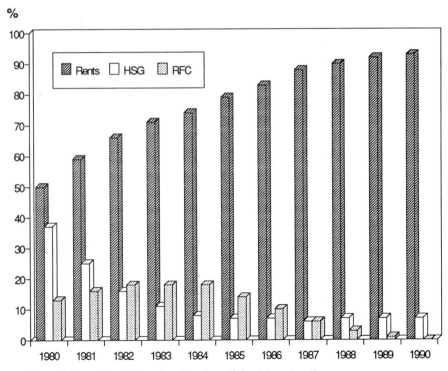

Figure Two: The Changing Profile of the Housing Revenue Account 1979-1990 *Source: COSLA, 1991, Annex 4*

For those on a steady but low income, the Right to Buy will seem financially more attractive. Already in many local authority districts the cost of servicing a mortgage on a discounted council house purchase is less than the rent being charged. Further, if rents rise significantly then the gap between the District Council and the alternative providers of rented housing in the so called 'independent' rented sector will be narrowed. If rent differentials are narrowed the attraction of switching landlords to gain an improved, or modernised, house will undoubtedly be enhanced. Subsequent transfers would only act to further polarise the situation for those tenants who remained.

That said, it is also worth pointing out that the emphasis of this legislation is heavily focused towards urban local authorities, with significant amounts of council housing. Scottish housing legislation has a tendency to be almost exclusively focused towards urban districts, with Glasgow typically being very much to the fore. The Housing (Scotland) Act 1988 is no exception. As a result, it is unlikely that there will be any real change in the amount of council housing available for rent within smaller, more rural districts. If anything Right to Buy sales, which have traditionally been far larger in the rural areas, will start to tail off. With limited subsidy coming from the Government, and income almost solely dependent upon rents, these local authorities are likely to have greater leeway in determining their own priorities. In such cases, local authorities may well be able to provide a better quality of service. It will, however, be very unlikely that they will be able to provide more housing for rent.

For the tenants of Scottish Homes, and those of the New Town Corporations the opportunity to remain with their current landlord is clouded with uncertainty. Although Scottish Homes initially gave a commitment to retaining a strong landlord section, their actions reveal a different set of priorities, as was noted earlier. Tenants of the New Town Corporations also face uncertainty as they move towards 'wind up'. Originally it had been expected that the New Town Corporations' housing stock would transfer automatically to the local authorities. That is no longer an option given the Government's strong desire to reduce the overall level of public sector housing within Scotland. Tenant opinion is, however, strongly supportive of the original transfer option, as witnessed by opinion polls in all five New Towns.

Initial talk of management 'buy-outs' has for the time subsided. Proposals now on the agenda focus on a reworking of this idea through the establishment of housing trusts. These organisations would take over the management of the New Town housing stock, with the long-term objective of taking over actual ownership. This option parallels what happened to the ex-SSHA stock in the borders, following the establishment of the Waverley Housing Trust.

The fact that the individual New Town 'wind ups' are to be staggered over the next ten years has acted against a strong unified tenants' campaign opposing these proposals. The high level of owner occupation now present within the New Towns has also been detrimental in this respect. Given that the Government has stated a desire to expand housing choice their opposition to the inclusion of local authorities as a future landlord option seems highly inappropriate.

TENANT'S CHOICE

Having already outlined the background to Tenant's Choice, focusing in particular upon the financial drawbacks which could confront local authorities in operating these new procedures, it is worth examining how popular it will it be with tenants. From the tenants' perspective there are two major drawbacks to getting involved with Tenant's Choice. The first is that if they choose to exercise the procedures, they automatically switch from a secure to an assured tenancy. As was noted earlier, this has implications in regard to their future statutory rights. The loss of the Right to Buy and limitations on the right of succession are the most obvious examples. Their inclusion can, however, be negotiated between landlord and tenant, as illustrated by the development by housing associations of the 'Model Assured' tenancy. The assured tenancy also alters quite substantially the grounds upon which an eviction can be legally pursued. Finally, the procedure for setting future rent rises alters as rents will be freely negotiated between landlord and tenant.

The second major drawback relates to the availability of landlords who are willing to offer this receiving facility. To ensure that landlords involved in the Tenant's Choice procedures are acceptable organisations, Scottish Homes has laid down a set of criteria which landlords must meet before they can gain 'approved' status. In the document *Guidance on the Criteria for the Approval of Tenant's Choice Landlords*

(Scottish Homes, 1989a) it states there will be a rigorous assessment of all those who apply. Landlords will have to display both experience and the skills necessary to provide a good housing service, as well as the financial resources for the continued management and maintenance of any houses transferred. Further, prospective Tenant's Choice landlords will also have to show a commitment to providing a quality housing service to their tenants.

The Waverley Housing Trust, described as a non profit making housing organisation, was the first to receive Approved Landlord Status in February 1990. The then Chairman of the Waverley Housing Trust was Michael Ancram, the ex-Scottish Office Housing Minister and until recently, a Board Member of Scottish Homes. This organisation had an arrangement with Scottish Homes to manage their stock in the borders, which had been agreed in the dying days of the SSHA. From its inception the Waverley Housing Trust stated it would encourage not only these tenants, but those of the various Borders local authorities to make use of Tenant's Choice procedures. It recently acquired the bulk of the Borders Scottish Homes stock following a voluntary transfer ballot. Tenant's Choice procedures were not employed.

A second approved landlord, namely Eildon Tweed Valley Housing Association, was established in direct response to the Waverley Housing Trust. This non-registered housing association is a wholly owned subsidy of Eildon Housing Association. It operates the same Scottish Homes management contract as the Waverley Housing Trust did on what were 120 ex-SSHA houses in the Tweed Valley. No decision has been made on transferring the ownership of these houses to date. Two other Scottish housing association have Tenant's Choice approved landlord status, these being West of Scotland and Langstane in Aberdeen.

The only other housing organisations which are proposing to make use of Tenant's Choice procedures are the seven fully mutual co-operatives which have formed within Scottish Homes stock in Grampian Region. These co-ops, once established, will buy management services from Grampian Homes, a private management company limited by guarantee. The majority of Directors of this company are to be tenants of the seven fully mutual co-ops, which are also registered housing associations. It is this organisation's intention to use Tenant's

Choice procedures to acquire ownership of the housing stock in their area on an individual basis (Robertson, 1991). As fully mutual co-ops, who wish to gain the financial advantages of MIRAS on a collective basis, they require all members to be tenants and all tenants to be members. Those Scottish Homes tenants who do not wish to transfer will continue to be managed by Scottish Homes in the interim.

Given that there are but three approved landlords to date, and that operations focus in Borders and Grampian Regions, for the vast majority of Scottish tenants there is no possibility of exercising choice through this mechanism. Although the approval of more landlords will undoubtedly ease this difficulty, the fact that so few have sought registration to date may reflect a general lack of interest in this scheme. Part of the problem, from the landlord's perspective, may be the fact that Tenant's Choice is an individual right. Consequently, the portfolio of property acquired in this way is likely to be very haphazard and scattered. This does not make for efficient and cost effective management. Being involved in large scale voluntary transfers would clearly be a far more attractive proposition. The Waverley Housing Trust clearly came to this conclusion. Overall, therefore, the likely use made of the Tenant's Choice mechanism may prove to be minimal.

VOLUNTARY TRANSFERS

As was mentioned earlier, the Government, realising that a reliance upon individual transfers through Tenant's Choice procedures would perhaps not result in their policy objectives being met, opted to encourage public sector stock disposals to other agencies. Under the Housing Act 1988 (the equivalent housing legislation covering England and Wales, but which also includes certain clauses covering Great Britain as a whole), future stock transfers can only now take place if the Secretary of State is satisfied that a due level of consultation has taken place and that the majority of those affected do not oppose the proposed transfer. Yet, as was also noted earlier, the SDD information paper *voluntary transfer of Local Authority Housing to Private Bodies* (SDD, 1988b) and a follow-on document *Scottish Homes: Procedures for considering Voluntary Disposals of Stock* (Scottish Homes, 1989b) gave the impression that much of the initiative for such transfers lie with the public body, whether that be a local authority, New Town Corporation or Scottish Homes itself. Further, given that in the majority of cases those involved in voluntary transfers will require Scottish Homes funding for acquisition and future improvements, this organisation will clearly have a substantial influence upon the transfer process.

Voluntary transfers therefore raise an interesting set of questions about the true extent of choice for tenants. Will the initiative for voluntary transfers come from the tenants themselves, Scottish Homes, or their respective landlords? For example, it may well be the case that a District Council, conscious of its own financial difficulties, may decide to adopt a policy of encouraging voluntary transfers. Given the substantial management costs associated with running certain un-popular estates, a low or even negative transfer price could be finan-cially attractive to the District Council in the long term.

With the 'wind up' of the New Towns presently on-going, the issue of voluntary transfers to a range of landlord organisations has already been well aired within Development Corporation circles. Further, *Scottish Homes' Strategic Investment Plan* (Scottish Homes, 1989) envisages a stock reduction, through voluntary transfers, of 8,817 houses between 1989 and 1993. Given that the financial structure of Scottish Homes is crucially linked to generating sales receipts, so that it can fund a substantial proportion of its enabling functions, there are strong organisational pressures for such transfers to take place.

Another pressure for initiating such transfers will be Scottish Homes itself. The main function of the enabling division, as opposed to the landlord division, is to bring about tenure diversification within large peripheral council housing estates. As was noted earlier, its first and third funding priorities are Partnership Areas and Community Renewal respectively, both of which are inextricably linked to the transfer of housing stock out of the public sector. For Scottish Homes to meet its policy objectives stock transfers have to take place. From what has been said above, it is clear that tenant pressure may not be the sole motive for such a transfer to take place.

As with Tenant's Choice those who opt to transfer to a new landlord automatically move on to an assured tenancy. The only difference is that those who transfer through the voluntary transfer mechanism will retain the Right to Buy. Given the potential financial repercussions of this for the new landlord, compensation is to be provided in the price paid for the transferred stock. Again it will be the local authorities' asset base which provides the financial cushion for the new landlords.

It should be borne in mind that the Right to Buy entitlement, under the new landlord, will be affected by any improvement works which are carried out on the transferred properties. If, for example, £20,000 was spent improving the property then this outstanding debt would have to be paid back to the landlord before a sale could proceed. This could effectively nullify any discount entitlement for the first five years. Only after this statutory period has elapsed would full discount entitlement be available.

While the switch to an assured tenancy, with its marked reduction in statutory rights, will initially act as a major disincentive to those contemplating transfer, its importance is likely to reduce through time. This is because as assured tenancies become more common they will become more accepted. As examples of major improvement works to particular estates become publicised, there will also be an increased desire on the part of tenants to get similar work carried out on their homes. The desire for modernisation should not be underestimated as one of the key motives for tenure transfers.

A further point about large scale voluntary transfers is that there are clear restrictions regarding the landlords to whom tenants can transfer. District Councils, for example, are excluded from being receiving landlords under the voluntary transfer arrangements. For tenants of the five New Towns in Scotland, who previously believed their homes would be managed by the local District Council following the 'wind up' of the Development Corporations, this decision represents a major blow. Evidence from recent tenants' surveys in each of the five New Towns indicated that the vast majority would prefer that their homes be managed by the local District Council. If the Government's motivation is to extend tenants choice then this restriction would seem to run counter to such an objective. This further suggests that ideological considerations take precedence over the stated objective of extending choice.

It is also the case that voluntary transfers offer tenants the choice of only one landlord. The switch of tenure can only be achieved through a single new landlord, whether that be a housing association, co-operative, private trust or private landlord. Further, if tenants do not like their new landlord they cannot opt for a second transfer. Again the concept of choice is clearly restricted, if not illusionary. Arguably the extension of choice is not the sole motivation of Government policy. The prime motivation seems more attuned to reductions in the scale of public sector renting within Scotland.

A recent development, related to voluntary transfers, is also worth commenting upon, particularly given its implications for both Scottish Homes and New Town housing stock. This is where a management contract is negotiated with a private company to manage publicly owned housing stock and that, in time, the company comes back with proposals to acquire the ownership of this stock. Although, to date, there has been but one example of this in Scotland, namely the controversial acquisition by the Waverley Housing Trust of Scottish Homes' stock in the Borders, there are currently two further bids being processed for management contracts of Scottish homes stock in Midlothian and Lanarkshire. These are for all intents separate management 'buy-outs' proposals, an arrangement which has also been discussed in East Kilbride.

As described elsewhere (see section on Private Housing Trusts) Scottish Homes stock in the Borders was transferred, after a ballot, to the Waverley Housing Trust. This stock had previously been managed under contract by the Waverley Housing Trust's associated private management company, Waverley Housing Management Limited. The contract was not tendered, but negotiated between Waverley Housing Management Limited and the SSHA, during the dying days of that organisation.

Before the end of this three year management contract the Waverley Housing Trust put forward a proposal to Scottish Homes to purchase this housing stock. Following requests by Scottish Homes two other organisations came forward with competing bids. These, by Link Housing Association and the locally based Eildon Housing Association, were then considered along with the Waverley bid by Scottish Homes. The two other bidders were, however, debarred from talking to the tenants, and only after protracted discussions with Scottish Homes were they allowed to survey a sample of properties to calculate future maintenance requirements.

As part of a consultation exercise a private consultant was appointed by Scottish Homes to offer independent advice to its tenants. After considering the competing bids, and the results of deliberations with tenants, Scottish Homes came to the conclusion that the tenant's best interests would be best served by the Waverley Housing Trust taking over the stock. Part of the justification for this decision was that, not surprisingly, the organisation best known to tenants was Waverley. The Waverley bid was not the highest, setting an interesting precedent in that the purchase price of Scottish Homes stock, subject to transfer, need only reflect the bidders perceived rental value and not that calculated by the District Valuer. This issue is currently being investigated by the National Audit Office.

Having concluded the bidding stage of the transfer, Scottish Homes then organised a ballot of the affected tenants. The ballot, run independently by the Electoral Reform Society, offered only one landlord option which tenants could either accept or reject. Scottish Homes were incidentally debarred by the Electoral Reform Society from including a leaflet in the postal ballot paper explaining why the Waverley bid should receive the tenant's support. Rather than organising the ballot over the whole stock it was broken up into 12 sub-divisions. Not surprisingly the ballot overall showed two thirds in favour of the transfer, one third against. All but one of the sub-divisions showed a majority supporting the transfer. The tenants in part of the Tweedbank estate, who rejected the Waverley option, are now managed by the Scottish Homes Dalkeith Office in Midlothian, some 50 miles away. Previously they had been factored by the local District Council. The tenants who voted against, but who were in sub-divisions where the majority accepted the Waverley option, were still transferred, even although the Government is on record stating that no Scottish Homes tenants would be transferred against their will.

This episode raises a number of questions about the voluntary transfer procedures, as operated by Scottish Homes. In the first place will the success of achieving a management contract eventually lead to ownership of that stock, given the advantage this gives in developing a transfer bid in terms of time, information and tenant contact? Given that tenants have no right to challenge a management contract, in that it covers management and not ownership, this could effectively act to reduce their future landlord options. Is it acceptable for Scottish Homes to act as judge, jury and promoter of the stock transfers within its own stock? Again tenant's choice is severely constrained in this context, if it exists at all. Is it the interests of tenants, or those of

Scottish Homes, which take precedence in such deliberations? Was the fact that Waverley could not get access to high levels of subsidy from Scottish Homes not a crucial deciding factor, given the organisations current weak financial position? Will Scottish Homes' staffing considerations not lead them to favour a management 'buy-out' option, rather than one from other housing providers?

Finally, is it ethically correct for Scottish Homes to pay private consultants to provide so-called 'independent' advice to their tenants, when they are actively pursuing stock transfers? Surely only when these advisors are paid by the tenants themselves can they truly receive independent advice on future landlord options, if such advice really can exist. The issue of independent advice is also pertinent to local authorities who actively promote voluntary transfers of their housing stock. It is therefore not surprising that Scottish Homes is currently reviewing all its procedures in relation to the voluntary transfer of its own housing stock to other landlords.

Types of Landlord   6

Given that voluntary transfers are likely to be the main focus for tenure changes out of the public sector it is worth examining the types of landlord that will be available to tenants contemplating such an option. The four types of landlord discussed in this section are private landlords, private housing trusts, housing associations and housing co-operatives. These four types split into two broad categories, namely private and voluntary housing association.

PRIVATE LANDLORDS

Private landlords let houses for profit. This is their main distinguishing feature. Broadly speaking, existing private landlords fall into two main groups. The first of these are either individual or small property companies, often long established, who let property within older tenemental districts. Within this sector are a group of landlords who specialise in providing furnished accommodation, often in multi-occupation. Although small in terms of the number of properties they manage, it is important to bear in mind that they house many people most of whom are very vulnerable. Rent levels for such accommodation are usually tied into the current DSS regulations. It is this group of private landlords who are constantly being accused in the press of sharp practice, profiteering and abusing tenants' rights.

The second broad group comprises newly formed companies which are either off-shoots of building societies, such as Quality Street, or companies formed specifically to take advantage of the Business Expansion Scheme (BES). Quality Street has recently announced however, that in the coming year, it is to formally break its ties with the Nationwide Anglia building society and buy up its shares which are held by the society. BES is a means whereby the Government offers enhanced tax incentives to small investors in order to focus investment into particular activities (Gibb and Kearns, 1989). These corporate private landlords let new or recently converted properties at high rents, often competing with hotels for the long term business executive market within large cities. The recent down turn in the housing market has reduced the attractiveness of this type of investment. These tax incentives were designed to operate for five years only, and their withdrawal in 1993 was confirmed in the 1992 Budget.

Private landlords do not have a good reputation in Scotland. To some extent the excesses of private landlordism have become very much part of Scottish folklore. This is undoubtedly related to the fact that one of the main pillars in the development of the Labour Party in Scotland centred upon campaigning for better housing. This in effect became associated with a staunch ideological opposition to private landlordism. Private landlordism provided the obvious focus for such campaigns, given the poor quality of accommodation offered and the often obvious exploitation of tenants. With the private landlord in terminal decline prior to the First World War, due in part to the lack of an economic return from this type of activity, the landlord's only means of maximising profits was through cutting back on repairs and maintenance.

The end result of this was the development of a reputation for both exploitation and squalor. The polarisation of political attitudes toward housing issues within many Scottish local authorities ensured this exploitative image became almost institutionalised. For many, the only solution to Scotland's housing crisis was the destruction of private landlordism, and its replacement by modern publicly owned housing stock. Many landlords, at the same time, sold out to owner occupation, anxious to gain something from their deteriorating and depreciating property. Caught in this trap the private landlord lobby found no support from the public purse to fund the necessary improvement works on their properties. Private landlordism as a tenure lacked any credibility with those who determined Scotland's housing policy. In part, this reflects their much diminished political influence, a process which started well before the First World War (McCrone and Elliot, 1989). The revival of the private landlord has, therefore, not been on the political agenda for decades. That said, Conservative philosophy has ensured the topic has been well debated, if not in fact included within practical policy objectives.

Given this history of decline and the public hostility towards private landlords, what are the prospects for this group taking over public sector housing stock? The answer to this question must be "extremely limited". In the first place individual landlords are not geared up financially to attempt such an exercise. Their reputation with the public is also very poor. They are equated with DSS bed and breakfast establishments and recent publicised court cases, such as the Norman Properties saga in Glasgow. In this case the landlord let uninhabitable property to young vulnerable people, at extortionate rents. Such cases have done little to improve the landlords' public standing. If anything the Norman Properties court case, and various Shelter campaigns, have acted to reinforce their exploitative image. As a result, public sector tenants would be highly reluctant to exercise Tenant's Choice to these organisations. Further, local authorities, and other public sector agencies such as the New Towns and Scottish Homes would also be highly reluctant to be involved in a transfer to 'cowboy' landlords.

Transfers to the new breed of corporate landlords are also unlikely to take place on a large scale. In the first place the landlord's image is difficult to reverse even through issuing impressive glossy public relations material. Secondly, at a more practical level, the commercial landlords do not view the management of ex-council stock as a financially viable proposition, unless access is gained to substantial levels of public subsidy. Paul Mugnaioni, the Director of Quality Street, has gone on record stating that better subsidies for the 'bricks and mortar' are required as well as an improved Housing Benefit system (Quality Street Ltd, 1989). To provide housing within what Quality Street calls the socially rented sector Mugnaioni has made a case to Government for his company to receive one-off grants similar to those being received by housing associations. The introduction by Scottish Homes of GRO Grants is, in part, a response to this demand. Mugnaioni, along with many others, has also called upon the Government for a marked improvement in the Housing Benefit system so that those on low incomes can afford to rent his property. At present the cheapest Quality Street rent, for a two bedroom property, is between £60 and £80 per week. Clearly, this is well beyond the reach of low paid council tenants. If private landlordism, at least in the short term, is unlikely to feature as an alternative landlord option it would be useful to examine three other types of landlord who have access to varying levels of public support.

PRIVATE HOUSING TRUSTS

The concept of a Private Housing Trust is extremely flexible. As a result it could be made to look much like a housing association with, for example, tenants on its board of management. It could also, for all intents, be a private housing organisation almost indistinguishable from a private landlord. Towards the end of the 1980s, with the new housing legislation producing much speculation and debate about the new types of landlord that could emerge, the idea of housing trusts received much currency especially in Institute of Housing circles (McGurk,1988).

The essential features of this envisaged new generation of Trusts, as envisaged within the current context of Government policy, are that they must be independent of the District Council; be bound by some form of Deed of Trust which defines certain social objectives; and be non profit making. Although the non profit making aspect is meant to distinguish them from private landlords, it should be pointed out a Trust can make a substantial surplus. The same is also true for housing associations. It is also the case that the two other constitutional criteria listed above could easily be accommodated by most housing associations. This, therefore, begs the question, what is different about a Trust?

Housing Trusts could choose to trace their history from the abortive nineteenth century philanthropic housing movement. At that time state intervention in the housing market was an anathema, so these organisation were established to show that people would invest in good quality housing for rent and in turn receive a low, but steady return on their investment. This idea failed even with significant indirect subsidies from both local and central Government in some cases. Most major cities at the turn of the century had a Housing Trust. Glasgow, for example, had its own City Improvement Trust from 1866. Those which survived beyond the First World War became part of the voluntary housing association movement.

In England and Wales, where the Housing Trust idea has created a great deal of interest within housing circles, if little concrete on the ground, they are seen as a means of fulfilling many of the objectives of council housing, while being free of the key constraints imposed by Government. For example, Trusts are regarded as 'private' and therefore are not subject to any restrictions on capital spending. As a result, Trusts are able to raise private funding as long as they service such debts and have an asset base to guarantee such a loan. Secondly, Trusts have more freedom to engage in commercial and investment activities connected with their objectives. Thirdly, if a Trust was established within a council estate future tenants would lose the Right to Buy thus preserving a stock of socially rented accommodation.

Under the new financial regime, heralded in by the 1988 legislation, the same opportunities are also available to housing associations. Within this context, therefore, the exact constitutional basis of the Trust becomes one of its prime distinguishing features. In other words, who exactly controls the Trust and what are their stated objectives?

The models presented in England and Wales are for all intents and purposes management 'buy-outs'. They are, in essence, the creation of professional housing staff, who see an opportunity to break free from the constraints imposed upon them by Government legislation. They have often been given the opportunity to do so by those who, while sharing the Government's basic ideology, are unhappy with Government policy towards the management and control of council housing (McGurk, 1988). In such cases the Trust would be very much a professional organisation, run with the professionals' own interests very much to the fore. There would no doubt be attempts to have tenant representatives on the Board of Management, but it would be unlikely that such representatives would have a dominant influence. Other proposals, south of the border, have talked about establishing a Community Development Trust where the management committee would be composed entirely of local representatives. Such an organisation would, for all intents, mirror a housing co-operative or a community based housing association. Their structure, however, would have to be examined before such an assertion could be validated.

Housing legislation in England and Wales also allows the Government to propose the creation of Housing Action Trusts for run-down council estates. Before they can be established the proposal must be subject to a ballot of the tenants of that estate. The Government has proposed a small number of HATs in England, but so far only one has proceeded to a ballot. In this case, in Sunderland, the Trust was rejected by the tenants. Given the apparent level of tenant opposition it is unlikely that HAT's will be extended to Scotland.

Experience to date of Housing Trusts in Scotland has been confined to one organisation, the aforementioned Waverley Housing Trust. The most obvious feature of this Trust is its organisational structure. Waverley Housing, rather than being one entity, is in fact two separate, but related organisations. The Waverley Housing Trust holds title to the housing stock, yet it buys its management services from a separate private company, Waverley Housing Management Limited, which is profit making. Key personnel from the private company also serve on the board of the Trust. The Waverley Housing Trust and associated company is, therefore, interesting in that their combined constitution and organisational structure manages to bridge between non profit and profit making concerns. This holds certain attractions to those keen to promote a model which encapsulates the revival of the private rented sector by what could also be seen as a resident controlled and socially responsible landlord. The Housing Trust itself has tenant representatives on its board, as well as representatives of the private management company, both in official and advisory capacities.

The Trust as an organisation owns the bulk of what was Scottish Homes' stock in the Borders. This was the stock which the private management company previously managed under contract. Under this arrangement the company paid approximately half the rental income to Scottish Homes. Previously the local authorities who offered this service were paid a management fee which, in the case of Roxburgh District Council amounted to £21.40 per house per year. The local authorities were, however, also paid for any maintenance work carried out. That said, the Waverley arrangement was far better than the deal previously struck with the local authorities.

The Housing Trust with its charitable aims sets down policy for managing this stock, and then negotiates a management contract to implement this policy with its associated private management company. It is the private company which provides the management functions of allocations, rents, repairs, maintenance and improvement. The management company servicing the Trust is not charitable, but a profit making concern. Its six man board is dominated by professional staff, with only one tenant representative (Waverley Housing, 1990).

This structure mirrors the old private tenement management arrangement with a private trust owning various blocks of housing, for example in Partick, which were, in turn, managed for the trustees by private factors. The difference is that there was rarely such a close relationship between the Trust and factor. Trustees could, if they were dissatisfied with the service offered, dismiss the factor and engage the services of another organisation. It should also be possible for the Waverley Housing Trust to re-negotiate its management contract if the service provided proved unsatisfactory. Yet, given the close relationship between the two organisations this does not seem likely. Another scenario is that the Trust may demand a service which the private management company regards as unacceptable as it cuts into their profit margins. Again the close relationship may act against such an outcome. Yet, the idea of creating this tension within a housing organisation was seen as imaginative and something well worth developing. With the idea of competitive compulsory tendering for housing management services about to break onto the political agenda this is an issue which will take on greater prominence. For a variety of reasons, therefore, this model is likely to feature in future stock transfer proposals, particularly within the New Towns and Scottish Homes own stock.

For tenants faced with the option of a Trust, which could be a significant number, there is a need to decide whether it would not be more acceptable to establish an organisation which has management directly under its control. Such control would include the hiring and firing of staff; setting standards in housing management; and ensuring that the tenants' objectives are also those of the professional staff.

Whether it is also correct to give the impression that private Housing Trusts are an option which tenants can choose is also questionable. As was noted earlier, Scottish Homes tenants in the Borders did not opt to be managed by Waverley Management Ltd. They did have the chance to decide whether they wished to transfer the ownership of their homes to the Trust. But was it real choice, in that Scottish Homes effectively decided that only one option would be made available, in a ballot somewhat reminiscent of Soviet elections. If such a model is developed further, and that certainly seems likely, the Government's professed desire to expand choice will seem rather shallow.

Under the Housing Trust model private investors will, in effect, own the housing which is eventually acquired. This housing stock will be managed by a new breed of 'factors' who were previously employed as public servants. The Government, or more precisely its agency Scottish Homes, through this arrangement also neatly manages to solve a major employment headache by promoting the development of this new private landlord sector. It also, by denying these organisations the chance to register as housing associations, ensures they will not be able to draw upon Housing Association Grant. Only low subsidy levels in the form of GRO Grants will be permissible. As a result, these new private landlords will not be supervised and monitored by Scottish Homes. This could result in these organisations operating to standards of housing management which Scottish Homes, through their monitoring role, would not accept for housing associations or co-operatives.

HOUSING ASSOCIATIONS

Housing associations are voluntary organisations which build, improve and manage houses mainly for rent. The houses provided are for people with a wide variety of needs. These range from general family accommodation, through to sheltered housing as well as housing for those with special needs such as people with disabilities. Generally speaking Scottish housing associations are either concerned with providing special needs accommodation or are community based organisations involved in urban renewal. While some housing associations operate within a tightly confined geographic area others are active across the whole country.

Housing associations, as was noted earlier, now form part of the so-called 'independent' rented sector. They differ from private landlords in that they do not trade for profit. The fact that housing associations are managed by voluntary committees, and are typically small in size, with only a few having more than 1,000 properties, distinguishes them from public sector landlords.

The executive authority within any housing association is its management committee which is elected annually at the association's Annual General Meeting. It is this body which sets out the policies of the association and employs the professional staff to carry out these policy decisions.

Membership of a housing association is open to anyone who has an interest in the work of that association. To gain life membership an individual only has to buy a nominal share in the association, usually costing £1. Membership means that the member can attend, vote and stand for election to the management committee at the housing association's Annual General Meeting. In community based housing associations membership is normally restricted to people who live within the association's defined geographic area of operation. Membership of a housing association is not limited to the tenants of that association. In fact, only the community-based housing associations have significant numbers of tenant members. Within these associations membership is open to all residents, whether they be tenants or owners. Hence, community based associations are often referred to as resident controlled landlords.

Although housing association staff are employed by that organisation it is important to bear in mind that both the members of the association and its management committee receive no payment for the work they carry out. Theirs is a voluntary contribution. It is this voluntary aspect which distinguishes the housing association movement from other landlords.

Housing associations have been the major growth area in Scottish housing since the mid 1970s. The Housing Association Grant system, introduced under the Housing Act 1974, allowed for the dramatic expansion of the housing association movement (Maclennan and Kearns, 1989). High levels of Government support ensured that a high standard of property was provided at rents which, generally speaking, were slightly above the average for District Councils. As a result of the Housing (Scotland) Act 1988 the whole basis of housing association funding has altered. The Government was keen to see greater use made of private investment in the work of housing associations, ostensibly to provide more houses for the same level of public subsidy. These changes have had major implications, both for rent levels and the type of tenancy offered by housing associations.

In common with other landlords in the so called 'independent' rented sector all new tenancies issued since January 1989 have been assured. As a result, these assured tenancies have rent levels set by the housing association itself, rather than one set by the 'independent' rent officer under the previous Fair Rent system. The relationship between subsidy levels and rent levels will be examined in more detail in the next section.

HOUSING CO-OPERATIVES

The major difference between housing associations and housing co-operatives is that all members must be resident within the co-ops properties. In the case of a fully mutual co-operative all members must be tenants, or prospective tenants, and all tenants must be members. As the vast majority of Scottish co-ops do not meet this criteria they are, broadly speaking, similar to community based housing associations. Within a community based association membership is open to both tenants and owner occupiers, who are resident within the district. It is also not necessary for a housing association tenant to be a member of the association. This mirrors the position of the majority of housing co-operatives presently operating within Scotland.

As with other housing associations, co-ops do not trade for profit. They are also relatively small in size, with few having more than 300 houses. Most are formed, just like community based housing associations, by local people who wish to improve both the housing conditions and the quality of the environment, within their local neighbourhood. As with housing associations, co-ops are run by their membership, who join by purchasing a nominal £1 share in the organisation. This entitles them to attend the Annual General Meeting, stand for election and vote in the management committee which has the responsibility for the day to day running of the co-operative. Co-op members, as with those of housing associations, are not paid for the work which they carry out. Instead, they work voluntarily for the benefit of the co-op, thus forming one distinct part of the voluntary housing movement.

The original housing co-operative movement in Scotland consisted of a handful of very small organisations who often owned only one property. These organisation were formed by people who shared particular views on how to organise living arrangements and as a result the co-op became an extension of these views.

The idea of housing co-operatives within public sector housing was pioneered in Scotland by Glasgow District Council. Its initial moves in this direction were the establishment of tenant management co-operatives within its own stock. The first tenant management co-operative was established in 1975 in the Summerston district in a newly constructed council estate. This was followed a few years later with the Spiers Co-operative in Yoker (Munro, 1991). The tenants' desire to have some control on a planned modernisation programme was the prime motivating factor in its establishment. Today approximately 10 per cent of Glasgow District Council's housing stock is under the management of such organisations.

More recently, larger independent co-ops have developed within local authority estates. These co-ops were established to take over the ownership of housing stock previously owned and managed by the District Council. Not only have they organised the full modernisation of this stock, but they have also taken over responsibility for both the management and maintenance of that stock. To many housing professionals these co-ops are described as the ultimate form of decentralisation and participation, with the local community collectively taking on the full responsibility for their homes (Clapham, 1989).

The development of housing co-ops also seems to bridge the ideological divide between left and right. For the Conservative Party, housing co-ops provide tangible evidence of self-help while the Labour Party views them more in terms of a collective solution to housing problems. So, although both support them for differing reasons, this support may be opportunistic at best. A similar problem presently afflicts the community based housing association movement.

The development of the housing co-operative movement in Scotland is strongly focused within Glasgow. Glasgow's experience of both tenant management co-ops within their own stock, and their active promotion of community based housing associations, who act as the District Council tenement rehabilitation agents, helped sponsor the development of housing co-ops. Following initial discussions with tenant organisations in 1982 Glasgow District Council approved the funding of four feasibility studies, namely Calvay Crescent (Barlanark), Ballantay (Castlemilk), Broomhouse (Ballieston) and Wellshot (Cambuslang). The District Council later approved a further three feasibility studies in Priesthill, Southdeen (Drumchapel) and Possil. Developments have occurred in all the above areas except Wellshot, but not always in the way first envisaged.

Out of the above there are only three fully mutual co-ops, namely Possil, Rosehill and Southdeen. Originally Calvay, Broomhouse and Castlemilk East were to develop upon these lines, but, due to the Scottish Office's insistence that, in order to receive Housing Association Grant to fund the necessary improvement works, those three organisations had to adopt a standard housing association constitution. As a result, both constitutionally and financially the latter three are identical to community based housing associations. The only real difference is that while one rehabilitates pre-1919 tenements the other improves ex-council houses.

For the three fully mutual co-ops the funding package and constitution is different. Constitutionally, all tenants are members and all members are tenants. Financially, the purchase of property was funded via a building society loan, not a Government grant. Necessary improvements were financed not via Housing Association Grant, but from the District Council's Non Housing Revenue Account budget. In other words, because the housing stock was no longer in District Council ownership it could receive improvement grants which were fixed at 90 per cent of £13,800. That said, because this budget was tight in terms of the works required, attempts were made to raise more money through private sector channels. This proved problematic in that the Government took the view that if Glasgow District Council guaranteed these loans it would count against their capital allocation. In the case of Possil this difficulty was overcome by the then Housing Corporation making Housing Association Grant funding available.

With identical HAG funding arrangements being adopted for future schemes the financial distinction between these co-ops has become blurred. It is only the constitutions that now differ between the organisations (for more information on the developments in Community Ownership see Clapham, Kintrea and Whitefield, 1989).

Within the rest of Scotland a number of other housing co-operatives have developed in the last five years. Co-ops now exist in Edinburgh, Dundee, Perth, Paisley, Wishaw and Kilmarnock. As with those in Glasgow, although their constitutions may differ in relation to being mutual or non mutual, their funding package comes in the main through the Housing Association Grant regime administered by Scottish Homes.

This section has shown that there are similarities between private landlords and private housing trusts. It is also the case that alternative tenures in the shape of housing associations and co-operatives are very much variations upon the same theme. In tracing the development of housing co-ops in Scotland it is clear that for all intents and purposes these organisations, with certain subtle differences, fall very much within a housing association categorisation. It is also clear that housing trusts, depending on how they are constituted, could well mirror housing associations. That said, although the constitution of the Waverley Housing Trust gives the impression that it bridges both the private and voluntary sectors, the reality is that Waverley is a private landlord organisation. The real distinction between these two broad categorisations lies in regard to their funding arrangements with Scottish Homes.

7   Financial Realities

For any of these organisations to make a significant impact on Scottish housing they will require some level of Government assistance. Levels of funding for private landlords and trusts would not necessarily be compatible with either housing associations or co-ops, which are in receipt of Housing Association Grant funding. With this in mind Scottish Homes have developed the new GRO Grant system which provides for a maximum subsidy level of 30 per cent for private sector initiatives in the provision of housing for rent or sale. As a result, such issues as subsidy levels, acquisition price, availability of private finance and the likely impact of both these factors on rents require to be considered in some detail.

Having dealt with constitutional issues surrounding these various landlord options in the previous section it is now necessary to examine the financial environment within which these organisations will have to operate. This exercise will not only reinforce certain similarities between alternative landlords but it will also illustrate the central importance of Government subsidies to the financial well being of such organisations. The section traces recent changes in housing association funding, and the subsidy system which is available to each of these landlords. Of central interest is the impact these changes will have on rent levels. The section concludes by attempting to explore the complex debate surrounding the issue of affordability.

CHANGES IN THE HOUSING ASSOCIATION GRANT REGIME

To understand the full implications of the recent changes in housing association funding it is useful to compare and contrast the previous Housing Association Grant (HAG) system with the current system.

THE PREVIOUS SYSTEM

The Housing Act 1974 introduced the HAG system as a means of expanding the housing association movement. HAG represents a capital subsidy which is paid to a housing association on completion of a housing project. It is, as a result, a once and for all payment, which under the old regime covered all capital costs which could not be funded out of rental income, less running costs. The rent was set via the Fair Rent system by the independent Rent Officer. Having received the Rent Officer's assessment of what the Fair Rent should be set at, the housing association forwarded this information to the Housing Corporation (now Scottish Homes). The level of grant was then calculated by deducting the cost of management and maintenance allowances, and voids, from the Fair Rent. With the remaining income it was a straight forward task to calculate what size of loan could be raised and subsequently serviced. In the case of a rehabilitation project the loan period was fixed at thirty years, while for new build it was sixty years. The loan repayment was calculated by multiplying the remaining rent against an annuity factor. An annuity factor is a figure, derived from a set of tables, which is used to calculate mortgage repayments.

TABLE TWO

Calculation of HAG Under the Old Regime (July 1988)

Rehabilitation	£	£
Total Annual Rent		900
Less M+M Allowances	689	
Voids (@ 4 per cent)	36	
		725
Left for annual mortgage repayment		175
Cost of Rehab Unit		35,000
Less mortgage @ 9.5 per cent over 30 years		1,728
£175 x 9.87613446		
GRANT REQUIRED		£33,272
		(95 per cent HAG)
NEW BUILD		
Total Annual Rent		950
Less M+M Allowances	485	
Voids (@ 4 per cent)	38	
		523
Left for Annual Mortgage Repayment		427
Cost of a New Build Unit		42,000
Less Mortgage @ 9.5 per cent over 60 years		4,478
£427 x 10.48615589		
GRANT REQUIRED		£37,522
		(89 per cent HAG)

Having calculated the size of the loan the HAG required was then fixed. More often than not HAG levels for rehabilitation work averaged between 90 and 95 per cent of actual costs, while for new build it was slightly less. To illustrate the above points the relevant figures for a rehabilitation and a new build scheme are provided in Table Two on the previous page.

The advantage of this arrangement, for housing associations, was that almost everything that could not be paid out of the rent was covered by HAG. HAG covered the works costs and VAT (where applicable); professional fees to architects and engineers; and the VAT on them. To ensure that the housing association did not go overboard in relation to the project works costs there was a set of unit cost limits to which all schemes had to conform. At the same time rent setting was largely independent of the process, in that the Rent Officer set the registered rent with no regard to the cost of the project.

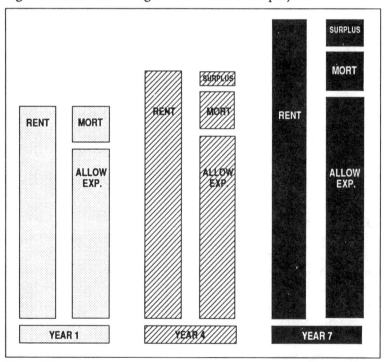

Figure Three:
The Creation of Surpluses under a Conventional Mortgage

In summary, the previous system can be characterised in the following way. Approval to proceed with a project was based upon a comparison with capital cost limits, not the current or running costs. The amount of HAG was not worked out until the project was finished and all the costs were known. HAG was not a fixed percentage of final costs, but the amount required to meet that share of the costs left after deducting a sum which the housing association could reasonably be expected to pay back by means of a mortgage. The actual amount of mortgage was arrived at by establishing the annual repayments which could accrue from the rent, less management and maintenance costs. The annual repayments serviced a fixed interest mortgage from the Housing Corporation, which was at a preferential rate of interest. This led to the creation of surpluses, in that rent levels increased over time while the loan repayments stayed fixed as illustrated in Figure Three. As a means of recouping these surpluses the Government introduced a 'claw back' mechanism called the Grant Redemption Fund. Finally, capital grants were made available for future major repairs and replacements.

As a mechanism for accelerating the growth of housing associations it was extremely successful. In the long term, however, the Government were of the opinion that it did not necessarily lead to 'financial efficiency'. By altering the housing association's funding system the Government sought to expose associations to risk and the rigours of the market. The method adopted to achieve this end was to reduce the level of subsidy and allow associations to borrow money privately to make up the difference.

THE CURRENT REGIME
The current financial regime has turned housing association funding on its head. While the previous arrangements could be described as rent led, the current regime is very much grant led. Whereas, under the previous arrangements, the rent in effect fixed the grant level, the new regime operates in reverse with the grant fixing the rent. While the previous arrangements protected standards, involved the association in little risk, generated surpluses and provided for major repairs, each of these aspects are still very much up in the air.

The last Housing Corporation Circular prior to the establishment of Scottish Homes spelt out the parameters of the current regime quite succinctly,

> *"In recognition of the greater responsibility which associations will have for their financial affairs, future applications for grant will require to properly address a wider range of issues in their presentation. Applications will require to encompass the capital and revenue requirements of a scheme, assessing the likely costs etc, and rent levels needed to service loans, provide for a proper level of management and maintenance, and build up a sinking fund for major repairs. Associations will also have to demonstrate that their proposals represent value for money in the context of achieving the stated objective."*

Source: Housing Corporation, 1989, para 6.

The basic, and most fundamental, change is that housing associations will now be expected to raise private loans to cover the difference between the HAG subsidy and the cost of the project. Whereas previously the average HAG was between 90 and 95 per cent, Scottish Homes was given an initial HAG target of 85 per cent. It is envisaged that the HAG average will reduce to 75 per cent within a four year period (Peschek, 1989). Clearly, if the amount of subsidy reduces, and the size of the private loan increases, there is likely to be a direct impact upon rents. Further, given that these private loans will be set at commercial rates of interest, not at the previous preferential rates, rent rises are likely to be even more substantial.

At the same time, by increasing the role of private finance the Government has effectively placed far more responsibility upon the housing associations. They now have the crucial responsibility to set rents. The independent Rent Officer no longer sets the rents for new housing association tenancies because these are within the deregulated assured sector. Rent Officers still have a role for tenancies which were started prior to the enactment of the 1988 legislation. It also follows that associations will be given more flexibility in relation to the quality and standard of housing they produce. There has also been talk about the associations determining their own management and maintenance allowance levels, although an early attempt by Scottish Homes to do away with centrally set allowances was abandoned.

Associations also carry the full risk in developing schemes, a risk which was previously covered by the Government. Instead of HAG being set at the end of a project, when all costs are known, under the new arrangements HAG is set at the start. Any cost overruns consequently become the association's responsibility, to be funded either out of reserves, rents or the sale of property. Only as a last resort will Scottish Homes provide grant to bail out an association. Finally, because under these new arrangements Major Repairs HAG has been abolished, all new housing associations projects must ensure that they put money aside into a reserve, or sinking fund to cover such works. These would include renewal of roofs, or other major elements outwith day to day or cyclical maintenance programmes. This additional cost also has a bearing on rent levels.

Just as the introduction of private finance necessitated a new form of tenancy, which limited tenants' rights and allowed for the free negotiation of rents between landlord and tenant, it has also had a profound effect upon housing associations. That said, it is the relationship between the amount of subsidy and the type of private loan that is of crucial importance, particularly in relation to rents. It would be worthwhile to explore this aspect in more detail, and in particular focus upon the likely impact of these changes on rent levels.

PRIVATE FINANCE:
THE IMPLICATIONS FOR RENT

Within housing associations, as with any other landlord organisation whether District Council or private landlord, rents must cover a set number of items. From what was said earlier, housing association rents must, firstly, cover the annual mortgage repayment. Secondly, an allowance must be made for void property, that is property which, for a variety of reasons lies empty for some part of the year. Thirdly, rents must provide for property insurance payments as well as the day to day and cyclical maintenance of the house. Finally, a proportion of office overheads and the full costs of the housing management staff must also be covered. What distinguishes a private housing organisation from other landlords is that on top of the above a profit element must also exist.

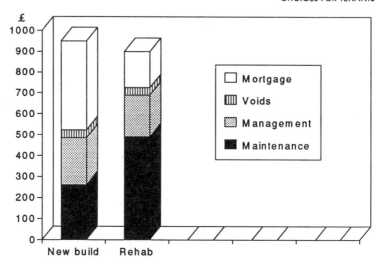

Figure Four: Elements of Rent under the Old Regime

To see the various components that have to be covered by a tenant's rent see Figure Four above. The examples provided cover housing association new build and rehabilitation projects under the previous HAG arrangements. As was noted in the previous section new build received, on average, a smaller level of HAG than rehabilitation. This was partly because it could attract a slightly higher rent, but, more importantly, the property was expected to require less maintenance. The fact that the mortgage, covering the residual loan, was taken out over sixty years, as opposed to thirty years for new build also contributed.

It was also noted earlier that the use of this conventional mortgage, through time, produced surpluses. This is illustrated by Figure Three, page 74. Under the current financial arrangements the level of subsidy was initially reduced to an average of 85 per cent, thus increasing the size of the private loan to make up the difference.

The size and type of loan is of crucial importance in determining the final rent levels. That said, however, the most critical element in determining the rent is the initial level of subsidy, as this determines the size of the private loan. Housing associations were originally encouraged to use low start finance.

"Associations developing schemes using private funds will generally be expected to raise long-term finance on a low-start basis, under which their repayment obligations increase over time in the same way as their income from rents. This will enable a higher proportion of scheme costs to be met through loan, and grant rates, accordingly, to be kept lower, than if conventional repayment mortgages are used. Use of conventional private finance, or a mix of conventional and low-start is not ruled out, but associations proposing such funding will have to provide full justification for this and offer clear and acceptable proposals for funding any increased cost which might result from their proposed financing arrangements."

Source: Housing Corporation, 1989, para 5.

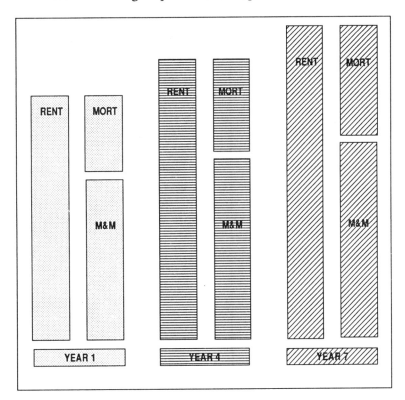

Figure Five: The Theory of Low Start Finance

Low start finance is designed to reschedule the repayments over time. Instead of surpluses building up, as with a conventional mortgage, the scheduling of payments ensures no surplus develops. As a result, mortgage repayments are lower at the start, thus allowing either a lower rent or a lower level of subsidy at the time when the project is initially completed. This is illustrated in Figure Five on page 79.

One consequence of using low start finance is that it is necessary to build in a sinking fund to cover major repairs. With a conventional mortgage the surpluses which accrue could provide an income to fund this work. The impact of a major repairs sinking fund on the eventual rent is quite striking, and this to some extent negates the benefits of low start funding. This is clearly illustrated in Figure Six below which compares the rent levels for a rehabilitation project under the old and new financial regimes. The consequences of 85 per cent HAG and the use of low start private finance could double rents if all other parameters stayed the same. Clearly, if standards were reduced, or maintenance levels cut, or allowances pruned, resulting rents could be further lowered. These elements are, however, unlikely to reduce rents

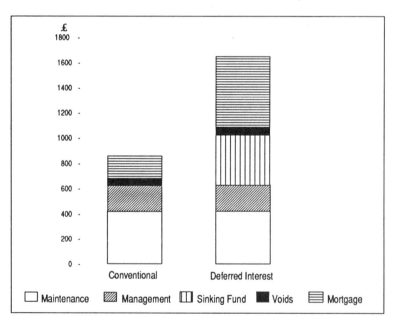

Figure Six: A comparison of rent levels under the old and new regimes

substantially but would, if adopted, reduce the standards expected of housing association accommodation.

In addressing this problem the housing association movement has forced a major re-think on the use of low start finance. This was undoubtedly aided by an accountancy practice which would have forced housing associations to account for full liabilities, including any interest which had been deferred. As a result private lenders would be discouraged as the level of liabilities could trigger default clauses in certain agreements (Housing Association Weekly, 1989).

That said, confusion about what level to set the sinking fund at, and the impact this had on rents were undoubtedly of critical importance in shifting Scottish Homes' preference away from low start funding. There was no agreement about what an acceptable sinking fund figure should be. Conventional funding has, as a result, become the more likely funding option for future projects, although there is a move to re-assert the low start option as a means of reducing HAG. While omitting the need for a sinking fund conventional funding results in higher repayments at the start of the loan period, the surpluses which accrue and the possibility of refinancing the property in a later period are thought to be sufficient to cover major repair works. There may also, however, be a need to re-examine the issue of Major Repair HAG.

As a reaction to obvious pressures on future rent levels resulting from the new financial regime, Scottish Homes and the Scottish Office have also engineered a means of redefining what constitutes the private element within a housing association's project. Unlike the situation in England and Wales, the Treasury will accept that home ownership initiatives within Scottish housing association projects can count against the HAG target. In other words, if an association does a certain proportion of shared ownership in a new build project, or improvement for sale within a rehabilitation contract, the receipt accrued from the sale will count towards the scheme's private finance component.

This arrangement also has the Government's ideological backing in that it helps develop mixed tenure, particularly within peripheral housing schemes. The problem from the housing association perspective, is that low cost home ownership initiatives are outwith the financial reach of their traditional tenants. Associations engaged in this activity could well be accused of turning their back upon their traditional client groups. It may, however, prove to be a necessary mechanism to allow projects to go ahead which will house the associations' traditional tenants. It is also interesting to note that where rent levels, for particular reasons, are higher there is not the same pressure to get involved in these tenure initiatives. Scottish Homes funding systems are therefore resulting in a geographically distinct development programme with housing associations in the West of Scotland being heavily involved in shared ownership while those in the East make more use of private loans financed by their higher rents. This is an interesting state of affairs for a national housing agency to contend with.

AFFORDABILITY

Rent setting, and the related issue of affordability, have become a central debating point within the Scottish housing association movement. Although a great deal is known about the different methods of rent setting, exactly what constitutes an affordable rent remains both subjective and in some cases simplistic. Acceptable rent levels have been defined in terms of a particular percentage of an average person's income. Unfortunately, the level of the base line from which these calculations are made, and exactly what these figures mean in terms of actual cash for particular householders have been avoided in this discussion.

Rent setting and rent levels were issues which housing associations took notice of previously, but did not necessarily play a central role in determining. As was mentioned earlier, rents were set by the independent Rent Officer following the Fair Rent legislation set out in the Rent Act 1965, with any appeal by the affected tenant being considered by the Rent Assessment Committee. Such an arrangement had both advantages and disadvantages. The advantage being that as the association did not have ultimate responsibility for setting the rent, blame for any rises could be focused elsewhere. The disadvantage was that the organisation, in not holding this power, was not necessarily master of its own destiny. The Government took the view that this arrangement did not necessarily produce efficiencies in terms of management and maintenance.

Under Section II of the Housing Act 1988, therefore, it gave housing associations the power to set their own rents. To ensure that housing associations set rents which are sensitive to the wealth within the local community, it has been considered essential by some associations that local income surveys are conducted. This action will also have the advantage of improving the quality of the debate on the whole issue of what constitutes an affordable rent. Justification for such an approach is found within the SDD's guidance '*Rent Setting - Housing Associations Publicly Assisted Housing*' where it states that '*associations should establish what their identified client group would be able to pay in rent*' (SDD, 1988a, para 5).

In a recent income survey for Whiteinch and Scotstoun Housing Association it was revealed that rent as a proportion of net income ranged between six and forty-eight per cent net. This figure included Housing Benefit payments (Heron, Robertson and Sim, 1990). On average, tenants of the housing association paid just over one fifth of their income as rent. Again Housing Benefit was treated as a source of income. The idea that a national percentage would simply define an affordable rent was, therefore, shown to be inappropriate because such an average would be difficult to achieve for all tenants. Given the high level of dependency upon State Benefits, reflected by the large rent / income ratios, the association's present rent regime undoubtedly poses difficulties for a significant number of its present tenants. Many of the association's tenants will presently be caught within the so-called 'poverty trap'.

The information on income levels should allow Whiteinch and Scotstoun Housing Association to set rents which are sensitive to the level of wealth within the community. Whether the Government's housing agency, Scottish Homes, will provide HAG at a sufficient level to allow such rents to be set is still to be tested. That said, given the income information provided by this survey, and the high proportion of income that is presently expended on rents, it is clear that the housing association has little scope to increase rents.

If the Government's intention is to reduce the level of public subsidy going into future housing developments, then the only means open to a housing association would be to cater for a different client group. This would not, however, meet with the objectives of either the housing association movement or the Government. Both agree that housing must be affordable to traditional client groups, namely those in housing need. When housing associations have determined what they consider to be an affordable rent, and established a rent policy to reflect their rent policy, it will be interesting to see whether Scottish

Homes concurs such interpretation, through the allocation of subsidies to new developments. It is the HAG level, after all, which determines the rent level.

Given the evidence from this study, and both the independent *Inquiry into Housing in Glasgow* (Grieve, 1986) and the SFHA *Who do we house?* study (Wilson and Alexander, 1988), it is reasonable to assume that housing association tenants are amongst the poorest in Scotland. The issue of affordability is crucial for the whole housing association movement. The debate can only be furthered by accurate, locally based income information. It is therefore encouraging to see the SFHA and Scottish Homes jointly working on the SCORE project which is designed to continuously monitor the incomes of all new housing association tenants. With this information, both at a national and local level, rent setting will undoubtedly be a more sensitive process. Whether Scottish Homes provides subsidy levels for projects which are sensitive to such income circumstance will be something to closely monitor. Income surveys, however, cannot in themselves reveal to housing associations or Scottish Homes what is an affordable rent. That is very much a political decision.

Conclusion 8

Through this examination of the various options arising out of the Housing (Scotland) Act 1988 it is clear that Government housing policy has moved beyond merely promoting owner occupation via the Right to Buy. Rather than being content with the pace of privatisation via this mechanism, the Government has opted for a second phase of the process through the creation of a quasi market within the provision of socially rented housing, outwith the local authority sector.

CREATION OF QUASI MARKETS

Crucial to this process has been the introduction of private investment into the provision of all new housing by housing associations and co-operatives. These two housing providers currently constitute the only credible organisations within the newly created 'independent' rented sector. The introduction of this private finance element into their work necessitated the creation of a new form of tenancy agreement, the assured tenancy. To some extent the introduction of direct private investment has moved the clock back to a time when this was the norm in the provision of rented accommodation, and tenants' rights played second fiddle to those of investors keen to ensure a return on their investment. By re-creating a role for investors within the provision of rented housing the Government hopes to foster the disciplines of the market. Thus a new vocabulary will shortly arise within housing circles whereby all future decisions will require to be measured against the concepts of economy, efficiency and effectiveness.

Value for money will undoubtedly become the new touch stone for all those involved in the provision of rented housing, whether they be housing associations, co-operatives and for that matter, District Councils. It will be interesting to try and ascertain exactly what parameters will be employed to conduct this exercise. The imminent arrival of competitive tendering for housing management services, which is in part a consequence of this legislation, will also act to sharpen this debate. Examination of other areas of public provision currently undergoing the introduction of quasi markets, namely

Education and the Health Service, vividly illustrates this point. Economy, efficiency and effectiveness, encapsulated under the banner of 'Value for Money' are fast becoming the principal considerations within their respective work areas. The lack of political debate on the privatisation of housing, as compared with other public services, illustrates only to clearly the demise of housing as a political issue within Scotland.

REAL CHOICE

Central to the Government's active promotion of the market mechanism as the most efficient distributor of resources, is the concept of choice. In housing, as within the Health Service and Education, the Government has made much of how their reforming policy agenda will expand choice. The White Paper, *Housing: the Government's Proposals for Scotland* (SDD, 1987b) contains much about expanding choice for tenants. Tenant's Choice, a new individual right for all public sector tenants, was initially envisaged to be the central plank of this approach.

Unfortunately, within any market system choice is very much related to the ability to pay. Where there is poverty, something only too prevalent within substantial tracts of Scotland's vast public sector estates, then choice is severely limited. Perhaps reflecting this the Government's housing legislation, in reality, offers very little real choice.

Choice is restricted by an individual's ability to pay. Given this fact a number of pertinent questions arise in relation to the Government's housing policy. In the first place will real choice only be available to those who can afford to pay in the future? The Government takes the view that rent levels are a matter best left to landlord and tenant to resolve. As a consequence Government has no locus on this issue. However, as illustrated earlier, the Government's housing agency Scottish Homes holds the key to future rent levels, as it determines the amount of subsidy available for individual housing association or co-operative projects. Scottish Homes, effectively, take a *de facto* view on future rent levels for both these organisations.

The recently agreed arrangement between Scottish Homes, SDD and the Treasury whereby low cost home ownership initiatives, such as Improvement for Sale and Shared Ownership, can be counted against the private finance element of future rented housing developments is a clear indication that Government does have some view as to what is an affordable rent. It is also an indication that the prospect of large scale private investment in the work of Scottish housing associations and co-operatives is not, at least in the short term, an attractive proposition to commercial lenders. If rents end up being too high then the Government will be unable to make their housing policies attractive to public sector tenants. They will not choose to switch landlords. That said, if the subsidy level is too high from the Government's perspective, then this will limit the number of transfers that can be funded. It is, therefore, very much a balancing act between future rent levels and the amount of subsidy Government is willing to make available. Scottish Homes' role is that of a juggler, trying to initiate change within these two sets of constraints. Choice from the tenants' perspective is consequently very limited.

The conventional view of choice, that of consumers having a variety of options from which to pick, shoppers selecting breakfast cereal from supermarket shelves, does not operate within this context. For most council tenants, in opting to transfer their landlord, there will be but one choice on offer, a housing association or co-operative. They will not get to choose from a range of options. Interestingly, given the lack of landlord interest in Tenant's Choice, individual choice in this regard is also not a realistic option.

For tenants of the New Town Corporations the choice of opting for District Council landlords is not to be made available. The same is true for Scottish Homes' tenants. In their case the choice of future landlords is likely to be both delayed and limited. In the interim, management companies which call themselves Housing Trusts are likely to appear. These new organisations, which for all intents and purposes are composed of the previous Scottish Homes or New Town housing management staff, will initially manage the stock under a contract with their old employers. The tenants will have no say in this arrangement since it involves the management, not the ownership of the stock. Only after the management contract has run its course, after two or three years, will the issue of ownership be raised. Only at this stage will tenants be offered the chance to decide whether they want their homes owned by these newly created Trusts. Yet, by this stage can this really be construed as choice? For all intents and purposes the Trusts' ownership of this stock will be a *fait accompli*. After all, will tenants be in a position to choose another landlord? This did not occur in the Borders. Will any other landlord be in a position to offer an alternative package given the central position Scottish Homes has in this process? Bear in mind that these landlords will have just fulfilled a management contract with Scottish Homes.

The reality of the Government's housing legislation is that choice is severely limited, and rarely exists at all. Real choice only exists for those who can afford to exercise such choice. Where the Government has a direct say in the future management of rented stock, choice is further limited because of over-riding policy objectives which have more to do with reducing the level of public sector housing within Scotland than giving individuals a real choice in selecting who their future landlord will be. Related to this objective is an attempt to re-establish organisations highly reminiscent of old style private landlord-ism, via what are effectively management 'buy-outs' of Scottish Homes and New Town stock.

It should also not be forgotten that for many involved in a transfer out of the public sector this will happen against their will. In any transfer there will always be a minority, and possibly a substantial minority, who oppose the transfer and the resultant switch onto an assured tenancy. For this group there is no choice.

The choice of a decent rented house from the public sector is also not an option for a growing number of people. A combination of the lack of resources made available for council housing, the loss of stock through the Right to Buy and the imminent transfer of significant amounts of other public rented housing will act to further reduce, choice within this sector. Rather than opening up choice, the Government could well be accused of reducing the available housing options for the most vulnerable members of the community.

ACCOUNTABILITY AND CONTROL

Over the last fifteen years there has been a strong policy move towards both establishing and promoting resident-controlled landlords. This process parallels, and to some extent contributes to another policy development, that of allowing the tenants' views to be heard within the management of council housing through the mechanism of tenant participation. It should be borne in mind, however, that although both developments have occurred concurrently they are not necessarily synonymous with each other. The creation of a resident-controlled landlord does not necessarily imply the organisation's endorsement of tenant participation.

Housing associations have long been criticised for being unaccountable organisations. They are, however, accountable to their management committees and the Government through the monitoring activities of Scottish Homes. Yet, whose interest does the management committee serve, and how accountable is a Government agency whose Board is appointed by the Secretary of State?

With the development of community based housing associations and co-operatives the criticism that housing associations lack accountability has been less easy to sustain, at least at the local scale. Management committees made up of local residents could, in practice, be more accountable to local people in regard to service delivery than many District Council housing departments. An organisation managed by local residents, with their interests very much to the fore, employing staff to carry out their policy decisions, should be more accountable locally than a large scale housing department.

It would be wrong, however, to ignore the influence of Government in relation to local policy making, given that all resident-controlled landlords are dependent upon Government funding for their development activities. Local authorities themselves are also very much instruments of Government policy. This fact ensures that Government sets particular parts of the agenda. The issue of the accountability of Government agencies is another matter.

Before touching upon that, it is worth considering accountability in relation to local authorities. There is an assumption, because local authorities are elected organisations, that their housing departments are automatically accountable to the public. While the theory of this may be sound, in practice the opposite tends to occur. For a number of years, local authorities have displayed a reluctance to make their housing services more accountable to those they seek to serve. With notable exceptions, local authorities have taken a long time to develop positive strategies towards tenant participation. The parallel development of decentralisation of housing management, particularly within large urban authorities, has been slow to progress. This is not to suggest that local authorities cannot become more accountable to their tenants. Tenant management co-operatives, pioneered by Glasgow District Council, offer tangible evidence of what is both practical and possible. Unfortunately, as these organisations are tied into local authority funding they are not always in a position to pursue their local objectives. The issue of accountability and control is something that all housing organisations need to strive towards. It is also an issue which the Government's housing agency could learn much from.

There was a time when such organisations were seen as public instruments of Government, working for the common good. Such organisations, although run by appointed boards, were still viewed as public servants. That perception has altered greatly in the recent past. As a result of the Government's desire to stimulate the disciplines of the market within these organisations they now exude the image of being quasi private sector organisations. The distinction between the public good and private gain inevitably becomes blurred.

Where this blurring is most acute is in regard to the disposal of Scottish Homes and New Town housing stock. The development of private sector housing trusts, staffed by people who previously were employed by Scottish Homes as housing managers, certainly does raise issues of accountability and control. Unlike housing associations and co-operatives these organisations would not have tenants taking on a management role. Rather their function would be that of token advisers to a private management company. Accountability for such private sector organisations would be to their investors, as opposed to the tenants they seek to house. Such organisations, therefore, represent a threat to the development of resident-controlled landlords. To portray such trusts as resident-controlled organisations is a sham. The Government, by promoting these organisations, seems willing to sacrifice the idea of resident control to that of control by the private financiers. This represents an extremely retrograde step. Unfortunately, it is a development which has more to do with protecting the employment of Scottish Homes management staff while at the same time ensuring that these new organisations cannot draw upon future subsidy support. It has little to do with improving either the quality of housing management, or the quality of stock provided. Competing policy objectives would seem to have blurred the idea of ensuring residents have greater say in how their housing is managed. Local accountability and control has gone out the window.

FINANCIAL CONSTRAINTS

The issue of finance is, of course, central to this whole debate. The Government, in attempting to ensure the limited resources they make available are stretched further, is keen to promote private investment in rented housing. Private investment, however, brings with it costs both in terms of rent payments and tenants' rights. The introduction of private investment brought with it the assured tenancy and the consequent dilution of tenants' rights. Private finance also brought the prospect of substantial rent rises. As was noted earlier, Scottish Homes, to ensure that the Government's housing objectives are met, has to juggle between the desire to reduce subsidy, on the one hand, and the consequent high rent regime that could result, on the other. To bridge this gap Scottish Homes has negotiated a unique arrangement whereby low cost home ownership initiatives count against the private finance element within any future rented scheme. The reality revealed by this solution is that rented housing, to be affordable, still requires anything between 85 and 90 per cent Housing Association Grant. All that has altered is the number of rented units that can be produced. For those in desperate housing need the chances of being adequately housed have declined as a consequence of this arrangement. Housing need, under this financial arrangement, now includes all those debarred from the owner-occupied sector because of high house prices. This is a very wide definition of housing need, a definition which has the obvious potential of discriminating against those in greatest need. That should not come as a shock, however, given that owner-occupiers in Scotland receive a higher level of subsidy than those who rent their accommodation. It is however galling that a Government which has preached against 'bricks and mortar' subsidies for the public sector should be so willing to support the very same subsidy system for the promotion of so called low cost home ownership initiatives by private developers.

TABLE THREE

SCOTTISH PUBLIC EXPENDITURE ON HOUSING TO 1992-93
(in £ millions)

CATEGORY	1989-90	1990-91	1991-92	1992-93
	£	£	£	£
Gross	1,109	1,024		
Receipts	453	376		
National Loan Fund	36	10		
Net	621	639	650	660

Source: Scottish Office, 1990, Table 15.5

The public expenditure figures, discussed previously, suggest that the Government is committed to reducing overall expenditure within Scottish housing (Scottish Office, 1990). The level of cut over the next two to three years will be anything between 18 and 30 per cent in real terms, depending on the level of house sales receipts received from all public sector sources (see Table Three). Scottish Homes' budget from Government, rather than expanding, as the Minister has chosen to portray it, has in fact been cut over the last three years. Only the high level of sales receipts, from the ex-SSHA housing stock sold under the Right to Buy, has buoyed up the organisation's income. This source of balancing finance has also declined markedly in financial year 1990-91 and 1991-92. If this trend continues, and with higher interest rates forecast there is no reason to suspect it will not, then the prospects for major transformation of Scottish housing, resulting from the Government's housing proposals, look extremely limited.

The National Loan Fund expenditure, in Table Three above, relates to a technical transfer of outstanding Housing Corporation loan payments, made under the old financial regime, to capital grant expenditure.

Many projects and initiatives, currently being discussed, will not be funded in the next few years. Local authorities who have just concluded partnership arrangements for future developments may in fact find that these do not come to fruition. Rather than looking to a period of growth, existing housing associations will have to accept decline. The prospects for the homeless, those who reside in housing suffering dampness and disrepair, those living on bleak peripheral housing estates, those living in inadequate housing in the rural communities, and those who require housing specially adapted for their needs, do not as a consequence look bright. To tackle these problems the Government has to give a major financial commitment. This particular piece of housing legislation does not ensure that this will occur. Rather it merely attempts to establish a new housing agenda which does not directly address the fundamental problems of Scottish housing.

Bibliography

Back, G., and Hamnett, C., (1987), 'State housing policy formation and the changing role of housing associations in Britain', *Policy and Politics*, 13, 393-411.

Brailey, M., (et al.), (1989), *Meeting Special Needs in the Community: An Introductory Guide for Local Housing Providers*, Integrate, Glasgow.

Bright, J., (1989), 'Second time around', *Inside Housing*, 6, 36, 8-9.

City of Glasgow District Council, (1987), *House Condition Survey, Volume One, The Condition of Glasgow's Housing*, City of Glasgow District Council, Glasgow.

City of Glasgow District Council, (1990), *Code of Practice on Voluntary Transfers*, Report of Housing Committee, 3rd October, City of Glasgow District Council, Glasgow.

Clapham, D., (1989), *Goodbye Council Housing*, Fabian Paper, Unwin Hymn, London.

Clapham, D., Kintrea, K., and Whitefield, L., (1990), 'The origins and development of community ownership in Glasgow', *Central Research Papers*, Scottish Office, Edinburgh.

COSLA, (1987), *Home Truths: COSLA's Housing Campaign*, COSLA, Edinburgh.

COSLA, (1991), *Observations on the Housing Support Grant (Scotland) Variation Order 1991*, COSLA, Edinburgh.

Glasgow Herald, (1989), 2nd, June.

Gibb, K., and Kearns, A., (1989), 'Business Expansion Scheme in Scotland: a framework for research', *mimeo*, Centre for Housing Research, University of Glasgow, Glasgow.

Grieve, R., (1986), *Inquiry into Housing in Glasgow*, City of Glasgow District Council, Glasgow.

Hamnett, C., and Randolf, B., (1988), *Cities Housing and Profits: Flat Break-up and the Decline of the Private Rented Sector*, Hutchison, London.

Hansard, (1990), Written Answer by Mr Lilley, Chief Secretary at the Treasury, 15 March, Column 375.

Heron, S., Robertson, D., and Sim, D., (1990), *Tenant's Income Survey: Report to Whiteinch and Scotstoun Housing Association*, University of Stirling, Stirling.

HMSO, (1971), *Report of the Royal Commission on the Housing of the Industrial Population of Scotland: Rural and Urban*, cd 8731, HMSO, Edinburgh.

HMSO, (1988a), *Housing Act 1988*, HMSO, London.

HMSO, (1988b), *Housing (Scotland) Act 1988*, HMSO, London.

House of Commons, (1984), *First Report from the Scottish Affairs Committee, Session 1983-84, Dampness in Housing*, Volume 1, HMSO, London.

Housing Association Weekly, (1989), 22 September.

Housing Corporation in Scotland, (1989), *Circular 3/89: New Financial Regime for Housing Associations*, Housing Corporation in Scotland, Edinburgh.

Hunt, S. (et al), (1988), *Damp Housing, Mould, Growth and Health Status*, Research Unit in Health and Behavioural Change, University of Edinburgh, Edinburgh.

Kemp, P., (ed.), (1988), *The Future of Private Renting*, University of Salford, Salford.

Mason, D., (1985), *Room for Improvement*, Adam Smith Institute, London.

Munro, T., (1991), 'The Speirs Co-operative Way', in Robertson, D., and Sim, D., (ed.), *Glasgow: Some lessons in Urban Renewal*, City of Glasgow District Council, Glasgow, 47-50.

Minford, P., (et al.), (1987), *'The Housing Morass: Regulation, Immobility and Unemployment'*, Hobart Paperback, Institute of Economic Affairs, London.

McCrone, D., and Elliot, B., (1989), 'The decline of landlordism: property rights and relationships in Edinburgh', in Rodger, R., (ed.), *Scottish Housing in the Twentieth Century*, Leicester University Press, Leicester, 214-235.

Mackay, G., and Laing, G., (1982), *Consumer Problems in Rural Areas*, Scottish Consumer Council, Glasgow.

McGurk, P., (1988), 'Selling the stock', *Housing*, 24, 3, 16-19.

Maclennan, D., (1989), 'Housing in Scotland, 1977-1987' in Smith, M., (ed.), *Guide to Housing*, The Housing Centre Trust, London, 671-704.

Maclennan, D., and Kearns, A., (1989), 'Public finance for housing in Britain', *Discussion Paper*, 22, Centre for Housing Research, University of Glasgow, Glasgow.

Nuttgens, P., (1990), 'Returning to the home front', *Search*, 5, 4-5.

Peschek, D., (1989), 'Shaking off the Thatcherite image', *Voluntary Housing*, April, 20-26.

Quality Street Ltd, (1989), *Annual Report and Accounts*, Quality Street Ltd, Glasgow.

Ridley, N., (1988), 'The local right, enabling not providing', *Policy Study*, 92, Centre for Policy Studies, London.

Robertson, D., (1989a), 'Attacking the dampness plague: Glasgow's response', *Health Promotion*, 4, 2, 159-162.

Robertson, D., (1989b), 'Landlord opens door to tenant's trepidation', *Observer Scotland*, 7th May.

Robertson, D., (1990), 'The traditional rented programme: a portrait of a dinosaur', *Discussion Paper*, Scottish Federation of Housing Associations, Edinburgh.

Robertson, D., (1991), 'No homes no more', *Housing*, 26, 2, 8-10.

Robertson, D., and McGregor, B., (1987), 'Rural housing in Scotland: an assessment of the issues', in McGregor, B., (et al.), *Rural Housing in Scotland: Recent Research and Policy*, Aberdeen University Press, Aberdeen, 9-16.

Rogers, R., (ed.), (1989), *Scottish Housing in the Twentieth Century*, Leicester University Press, Leicester.

SDD, (1987a), *Housing: the Government's Proposals for Scotland*, Cmnd 242, HMSO, Edinburgh.

SDD, (1987b), *Scottish Homes*, HMSO, Edinburgh.

SDD, (1988a), *Rent Setting - Housing Associations Publicly Assisted Housing*, SDD, Edinburgh.

SDD, (1988b), *Voluntary Transfer of Local Authority Housing to Private Bodies*, SDD, Edinburgh.

SDD, (1989), *Statistical Bulletin*, HSU No.7, SDD, Edinburgh.

SDD, (1990), *Statistical Bulletin*, HSU No.11, SDD, Edinburgh.

Scottish Federation of Housing Associations, (1989), *SFHA Interchange*, March, SFHA, Edinburgh.

Scottish Homes, (1989), *Scottish Homes Strategic Investment Plan*, Scottish Homes, Edinburgh.

Scottish Homes, (1989a), *Scottish Homes: Procedures for considering Voluntary Disposals of Stock*, Scottish Homes, Edinburgh.

Scottish Homes, (1989b), *Guidance on the Criteria for the Approval of Tenant's Choice Landlords*, Scottish Homes, Edinburgh.

Scottish Office, (1990), *Public Expenditure to 1992-93: A Commentary on the Scottish Programme*, Scottish Office, Edinburgh.

Scottish Office, (1992), *Statistical Bulletin, Housing Services*, HSG/1992/2, Scottish Office, Edinburgh.

Shelter, (1990), 'Mortgage repossessing and arrears in Scotland', *Press Release*, Shelter, Edinburgh.

Sim, D., and Brooke, J., (1984), 'Clearance in 1985, the experience of Barlanark in the 1980s', *Research Memorandum, 4*, City of Glasgow District Council, Glasgow.

Tenant Participation Advisory Service, (1988), 'Poor Scottish Homes practice in Glasgow and Shetland', *Tapestry*, April.

Waverley Housing, (1990), *Annual Review and Financial Statements*, Waverley Housing, Hawick.

Webster, D., (1989), 'A second class right to buy', *Housing*, 25, 6, 32-37.

Whitehead, C., (1987), 'The proposals for private renting: will the arithmetic work', paper presented *ESRC/Rowntree Housing Studies Conference 1989*, University of Salford.

Whitehead, C., and Kleinman, M., (1986), 'Private rented housing in the 1980s and 1990s', *Occasional Paper, 17*, Department of Land Economy, University of Cambridge, Cambridge.

Wilson, D., and Alexander, D., (1988), *Who Do We House, Interim Report 1987: A Survey of Tenant Housing Associations in Scotland*, Scottish Federation of Housing Associations, Edinburgh.

96